# *Finding Christ*
## IN CANCER
### A GUIDEBOOK AND DEVOTIONAL

To: Dawn Daughn

May Christ cheer your soul always!
(Psalm 94:19)

Love,
Katie Burnham

## KATHRYN BURNHAM PA-C

# Consolation Press

Oxnard, CA USA

*Finding Christ in Cancer:*
*A Guidebook and Devotional*
by Kathryn Burnham

First Printing – September 2013
ISBN: 978-1-60047-909-0
Library of Congress Control Number: 2013942946

The individuals and their cancer stories in this book are based on actual people; however, identifiable characteristics have been altered as a means to protect confidentiality.

Printed in the U.S.A.

0   1   2   3   4   5   6   7   8   9   10   11   12   13   14

*For Shawn,*

*whose love and*

*support never ends.*

# TABLE OF CONTENTS

# INTRODUCTION

"As for man, his days are like grass; he flourishes like a flower of the field; for the wind passes over it, and it is gone, and its place knows it no more" (Psalm 103:15-16). As a physician assistant in an oncology practice, I am reminded of this temporary life almost daily. It is what drives me to the Scriptures for answers, comfort, and hope. The result of my study is this book, *Finding Christ in Cancer,* which is written for Christians who have been diagnosed with cancer and for family and friends who are supporting someone with cancer. The goal of this book is two-fold. First, it is my ultimate objective to give encouragement from God's Word and His truths. Recognizing the sovereignty of God, His supreme authority on this earth, and the comfort He provides His children will strengthen the afflicted, thus allowing the cancer diagnosis to be reduced to a "trial," rather than a "tragedy." This book discusses the role of prayer, faith, and God's provision during a time of suffering and hardship, and it uses examples of biblical characters like Job, Paul, and David to demonstrate how we can best respond in a trial.

In addition to encouragement, this book will provide sensible and useful medical information which will help eliminate some of the fear associated with the unknowns of cancer. The medical information is meant to be answers to common questions and concerns, including the diagnosis and treatment of cancer, the likely side effects from treatment, and the implications of cancer on family and friends. By no means will this book give you everything you need to know about cancer—or replace the knowledge of an experienced physician. Hopefully, though, the combination of spiritual truths and practical information will serve as a guidebook for you throughout your journey. The end goal of this book is not to give false hope in modern science or cancer treatments, but to point readers to God's Word for hope in their present trials until they reach their eternal home with Him in Glory, whether their earthly lives are ended by cancer, or by some other means.

# CHAPTER ONE

# FINDING TRUST IN HIS SOVEREIGNTY

"You have cancer." These words are simple and few, but they have a very powerful meaning. They meant a lot to Carrie—a sweet, middle-aged college professor I met in the office about two years ago. She was admitted to the hospital for chest pain and cough and was released with a diagnosis of lung cancer. What transpired over the course of a few days in the hospital proved to be life-altering for Carrie and her husband. The shock of the situation combined with the many bits of important information can overwhelm even the most knowledgeable person.

Carrie had many questions about the cancer and the treatment. "How did I get this disease? What type of cancer do I have? What will my treatment be like? Will I be sick?" She needed clear answers to these questions and many more so she could make decisions regarding her care. For many years, the medical community has been criticized for insensitivity, failing to give adequate information, or not explaining the information in a clear way. Most patients I've encountered share similar concerns, so I want to clear up the confusion and give some answers to the most common questions about cancer.

## THE BASICS

Cancer is the repeated replication or duplication of a cell that has a mistake in its information system. Our bodies are composed of cells, and each cell has a specific task to perform. For example, a red blood cell is responsible for carrying oxygen to all the tissues of the body and a hepatic (liver) cell is responsible for eliminating toxins from the body. There are many different types of cells in the body, but the body requires all of them in order to work properly. The one thing all cells have in common, regardless of their role, is that they have the exact same information system, called deoxyribonucleic acid, or DNA. DNA is divided into small units, called genes, which tell the cell how to make a specific, and necessary, ingredient for it to function properly.

During a cell's life, there may come a time when the cell needs to make a copy of itself in order to have more workers for a particular task, or because the cell's life may be coming to an end. This process is called replication, and it involves copying the DNA so that the new cell will have the same blueprint as all the other cells in the body.

Unfortunately, throughout the cell's life, mistakes can occur in the DNA. Mistakes are also called mutations, and mutations can disrupt the entire function of the cell. During the process of replication, any mutation present in the DNA will also be copied if the cell has not corrected the mistake. When the cell continues to replicate multiple times instead of making only one copy, then the cell is cancerous. Uncon-

## I HAVE BEEN TOLD I HAVE CANCER. DO I NEED AN ONCOLOGIST?

The majority of cancers, such as solid tumor cancers like breast, colon, lung, ovarian, and blood cancers, like leukemia and lymphoma, are managed by oncologists. There are some cancers that can be handled by other specialists. For example, dermatologists care for skin cancers like squamous cell and basal cell carcinomas. They also handle very-early staged melanomas. Early-staged prostate cancers are handled by urologists, and early-staged thyroid cancers are handled by endocrinologists. If these cancers are diagnosed in later stages, or if they progress, then an oncologist will be asked to handle your care. Meet with an oncologist if you would like a second opinion. They are a great resource and can make sure you are receiving the best care.

trolled replication means hundreds, thousands, and millions of cells with the same mistake in the DNA. A cancer cell that no longer has the correct DNA blueprint will function separate from its original task in the body.

There are two major types of mistakes that occur in the DNA– acquired mistakes and hereditary mistakes. Acquired mistakes are those caused by outside influences, or environmental insults, while hereditary mistakes are those mistakes inherited from a parent. Inheritance is probably the easiest to explain. The entire DNA blueprint is tightly coiled into 23 pairs of chromosomes. Half of the information comes from the mother, and the other half from the father. If there is a mutation present in a parent's portion of the DNA before a child is conceived, then the mutation can be passed to the child.

Allow me to share Kim's story as an example of hereditary mutations. Kim made an appointment with an oncologist after her older sister was diagnosed with breast cancer. When Kim and her sister were younger, their mother died at the age of 45 from a very aggressive form of breast cancer. Kim wanted to know the likelihood of developing breast cancer, and she wanted to know what to do to prevent it from occurring. Kim also had two young daughters, so she was concerned about their risks of inheriting breast cancer.

Cancer in Kim's family was a result of the breast cancer genetic mutation called BRCA. BRCA-1 and BRCA-2 are genetic mutations linked to breast cancer and ovarian cancer. BRCA-1 is a mutation that occurs on chromosome 17, and BRCA-2 is a mutation that occurs on chromosome 13. "Patients with a mutation in either the BRCA-1 or BRCA-2 gene have risks of up to 87% for breast cancer and up to 44% for ovarian cancer by age 70."[1]

If a mother has the BRCA mutation, then she has a 50% chance of passing the mutated gene to her offspring. Fathers also have that same potential. Prior to any exposure from the environment, the child starts out with a defective gene on their chromosome. The corresponding gene on the matching chromosome from the other parent may then develop mistakes, make the attempt to repair, and become damaged over time. Unfortunately, the individual now has two damaged genes, so he or she develops cancer. As explained by The American Cancer Society, "Even when a person inherits a mutation, at least one more mutation is needed to 'knock out' the other copy of that gene (so that it doesn't function)."[2] People who inherit a defective gene will often develop cancer early in their life because they initially only had one good gene. This is one of the distinguishing characteristics of an inherited cancer—developing cancer at a young age, usually under the age of 50.

The second characteristic of a hereditary cancer is a significant family history of the cancer. Several family members may have breast cancer, such as mom, grandmother, or aunt, all because they carry the same genetic mutation. Men can also develop breast cancer because they can be carriers of the BRCA gene. However, male breast cancer is rare.

Although inherited mutations are easier to explain, they are not the most common type of mutation. Recall our patient Carrie, the college professor. Her lung cancer was not caused by an inherited mistake in her DNA, but by environmental insults to the DNA. The most common causes of mutations in the DNA are those induced by outside influences. Environmental insults, including chemicals, toxins, fertilizers, gases, viruses, and minerals, are those things we are exposed to in our everyday life, whether by choice or not, that can damage our DNA. These mutations damage the DNA of specific cells, rather than the entire genetic blueprint. Two common examples are cigarette smoke, which can lead to lung cancer, and ultraviolet sunlight, which can lead to skin cancer. Determining the exact cause of cancer may be difficult because we are exposed to many different insults on a daily basis. In fact, the exact environmental exposure that causes a cancer can rarely be pinpointed.

Interestingly, mesothelioma, a rare type of cancer that affects the lining around the lung, is a specific example where an exact environmental exposure is connected to cancer. The disease was first recognized in the 1870s, but it wasn't until the 1960s that J. C. Wagner and his team in South Africa studied a crocidolite asbestos mining community, and established a cause/effect link between asbestos and mesothelioma.[3] By June of 1960, Wagner's team counted 47 cases of mesothelioma with 45 of these individuals having been exposed to asbestos. Thus, the common link in these cases of mesothelioma was the exposure to asbestos, whether by directly working in the mines or by living in close proximity.

It took many years and, unfortunately, several cases of mesothelioma to occur before scientists were able to establish the link. Yet, not all the people exposed to asbestos in their jobs develop mesothelioma so there must be an additional component to developing cancer. The second component is due to the variation in the DNA. Certain genes may protect from cancers while others may predispose to cancer. Essentially, cancer development depends on the correct combination of environmental exposure and genetic material much like a lock and key system.

Cell mutations can occur quite often, but not all mutations will lead to cancer. In addition to an amazing information system, we were also created with amazing mechanisms to protect this system. In fact, it takes many mistakes before a cell becomes cancerous. Our DNA has the ability to repair damage through a complex and sophisticated system with many checks and balances. Our cells also have the ability to destroy themselves—a process called apoptosis—if they cannot make necessary repairs. As a result of these repair mechanisms, cancer development is not easy. Obviously, however, it still occurs.

TYPES OF CANCER

Cancer type is determined by the original cell that made the mistake. If the original cell was located in the breast, then it is breast cancer. If it was located in the lung then it is lung cancer. The same applies to colon and other solid mass tumors. Carrie was diagnosed with lung cancer because the original cell that became cancerous was a cell of the lung. Sometimes, however, cancers may appear suddenly in one location that was not the place of origin, and it may be difficult to determine which type of cancer it is.

In these cases, pathologists (doctors who examine tissues under the microscope) can often discern the cancer type based on certain characteristics of the tissue. Other times, they can only provide their best, educated guess. For example, several cancers can spread to the liver (breast cancer, lung cancer, colon cancer, etc.), so if cancer is discovered in the liver, then the tissue sample, combined with imaging studies, may be required to determine where the cancer originated

## HOW DO I FIND AN ONCOLOGIST?

Most insurance companies—especially HMOs—will dictate who you can see based on who they are contracted with. Even PPOs may have a list of in-network physicians where the insurance will pay more if you use someone from that list. If you are hospitalized when your cancer is discovered then you should know that not all oncologists will have privileges (the authority to see patients) in every hospital. Also, a referring physician may recommend certain oncologists based off of their own preferences and experiences.

before spreading to the liver. The cancer certainly could have originated in the liver, but liver cancer is not as common as breast, lung, or colon.

Leukemia and lymphoma are not associated with any particular organ; therefore, they are more difficult to understand. Leukemia is an abnormality of the blood cells and bone marrow. The bone marrow is the production factory for red blood cells, white blood cells, and platelets. There are several types of leukemia and different cells can be affected. Lymphoma is an abnormality of a particular type of white blood cell called the lymphocyte. Lymphocytes move around in a special type of fluid call the lymph system, and the purpose of the lymph system and lymphocytes is to fight infections that enter the body. Both leukemia and lymphoma can be diagnosed by a solid mass found in the body, or they can be discovered if the blood counts are abnormal. Leukemias and lymphomas are still considered cancer because the same definition applies. They are both caused by an abnormal cell that continues to replicate.

STAGING CANCER

Once the diagnosis of cancer has been confirmed then the next step is to "stage" the cancer. Staging the cancer will help the oncologist recommend the best treatment for your cancer. This is most commonly done through imaging studies like CT scans and

MRIs. There are four stages for each type of solid-tumor cancer and the staging criteria can vary with each cancer type. The staging is based on tumor size, lymph node involvement, and if the cancer has spread to distant locations. This is called the TNM (tumor, node, metastasis) system. With regard to staging, there are some very general characteristics that can be summed up in the following way:

Stage I. The cancer is localized to the primary site and is very small in size.

Stage II. The cancer is small to medium in size, and may have spread to a nearby lymph node.

Stage III. The cancer is medium to large in size, and has spread to one or more nearby lymph nodes.

Stage IV. The cancer is very large, has spread to the lymph nodes, and has spread to distant sites or other organs.

Stage I cancers are those that are small and located in one specific place—the site where the cell first became problematic. Cancer that has progressed to stages II and III includes larger-sized masses/tumors and also involve lymph nodes. When a particular cancer invades the lymph node, it is still the original cancer type and should not be confused with lymphomas or leukemias. The lymph system and lymph nodes are located throughout the body and are responsible for draining fluid from all the tissues of the body. Therefore, when a cancer cell is no longer localized to the primary site, it has likely moved to the lymph nodes that drain that tissue. For example, breast cancer often moves first to the axillary lymph nodes, which are located under the arm. Sometimes the difference between stage II and stage III is the location of the lymph nodes that have cancer involvement. If a distant lymph node contains cancer, then the staging is usually higher.

Finally, stage IV is the most advanced cancer, where the cancer has not

# WHAT SHOULD I LOOK FOR IN AN ONCOLOGIST?

Doctors are just like any other service provider. Some are very good at what they do, while others are not. First, look for someone who is knowledgeable and up-to-date. There are many studies and changes occurring in the field of cancer research, and your doctor needs to be constantly seeking that information, determining its validity, and changing his/her practice based on the evidence. This is the best way to make sure you are getting the currently accepted treatments. Ask your oncologist what the latest studies are for your particular cancer. We will talk about clinical trials in Chapter 7, but a good way to gauge a physician's current knowledge is to see if his office offers clinical trials to patients, either by directly coordinating clinical trials in the office or by referring patients to a facility offering clinical trials.

A second characteristic to look for is good communication. You may not like the news, but you want an oncologist who can tell you the information truthfully and accurately, and will be willing to answer your questions. A physician should give you his best advice based on all his knowledge. Oncologists know statistics, but, unfortunately, they do not know if you will be cured, or how long you have to live. A physician should guide you in the decision-making process, not make the decision for you, so pick someone whom you can trust to provide you with the best information so you can make an educated decision.

only moved to the nearby lymph nodes but has also moved to other organs or lymph nodes that are further away. When the cancer has spread to a different organ, it does not mean there is a new cancer present. It is the same type of cancer—just more advanced. For example, when an individual is diagnosed with lung cancer and the cancer spreads to the bone, the individual does not have a new bone cancer. The cancerous tissue in the lung will match the cancer in the bone, if both are compared under a microscope. The original cancer is now more advanced because it is no longer localized to the lung.

After discharge from the hospital, Carrie had a diagnosis of stage III lung cancer. The tumor was located in the left lung, but it had already spread to the nearby lymph nodes. She began chemotherapy in our office shortly after her diagnosis was made. I met with her and her husband on several occasions to discuss the treatment and the side effects she was having. She didn't understand how this could happen to her. "Only those who smoke develop lung cancer, right?" Carrie had never smoked. She didn't understand why it couldn't be removed surgically. She had met with a surgeon, but the surgeon felt like her cancer was too advanced for surgery. She was confused and angry, but mostly she was frightened.

ENCOURAGEMENT FROM THE WORD

*For as the rain and the snow come down from heaven and do not return there but water the earth, making it bring forth and sprout, giving seed to the sower and bread to the eater, so shall My word be that goes out from My mouth; it shall not return to Me empty, but it shall accomplish that which I purpose, and shall succeed in the thing for which I sent it.* (Isaiah 55:10-11)

Science and research have made many advances in the understanding and treatment of cancer, but even the best scientist or oncologist cannot pinpoint the exact cause of cancer, or the exact time it occurred. Many people can explain the replication of DNA and the effects of mutations, but that still leaves one questioning as to what caused the mutation in the first place. Oncologists can explain how chemotherapy works to kill cancer cells, but they cannot explain why some patients respond and others progress. More importantly, no one can predict who will respond and be cured, and who will die from their cancer. Carrie wanted to know why she had developed lung cancer, and the only certain answer I could give her was because God ordained it. If this statement shocks or concerns you, then please allow me an opportunity to explain.

Your cancer diagnosis may lead you to ask some of the same questions Carrie asked, and you may even be asking some of these questions to God. "Why me? Why now? Why here?" Though tough questions for any human to answer, these are simple questions for God. He has providentially chosen you for a specific purpose at this exact time and in this exact place. He knows exactly what caused your cancer, when it first occurred, and what the outcome of your cancer will be.

> He has providentially chosen you for a specific purpose at this exact time and in this exact place.

The sovereignty of God is part of our past, present, and future. It is the foundation for all events and circumstances in our lives. The sovereignty of God, also known as the providence of God, is clear in Isaiah 14:24-27, "As I have planned, so shall it be, and as I have purposed, so shall it stand...This is the purpose that is purposed concerning the whole earth, and this is the hand that is stretched out over all the nations. For the Lord of hosts has purposed, and who will annul it? His hand is stretched out, and who will turn it back?"

The New Testament also confirms God's sovereignty. In Ephesians 1:11, Paul writes, "In Him we have obtained an inheritance, having been predestined according to the purpose of Him who works all things according to the counsel of His will." Theologians David Steele and Curtis Thomas summarize God's sovereignty in this way, "All events, both small and great, come about as the result of God's eternal decree. The Lord God rules over heaven and earth with absolute control; nothing comes to pass apart from His eternal purpose."[4] Finally, Arthur Pink, in *The Sovereignty of God* gives Biblical references to prove his definition of God's sovereignty. "To say that God is sovereign is to declare that He is the Most High, doing according to His will in the army of heaven and among the inhabitants of the earth so that none can stay His hand or say unto Him, What doest Thou? (Daniel 4:35). To say that God is sovereign is to declare that He is the Almighty, the Possessor of all power in heaven and earth, so that none can defeat His counsels, thwart His purposes, or resist His will (Psalm 115:3)."[5]

God's sovereignty is shown throughout the Bible, starting in the very beginning and coming to full fruition in Revelation. As an example, God's sovereignty is clearly seen in the life of Esther. Though God is not specifically mentioned in the book, His hand weaved all the events, resulting in a glorious outcome. Some of these events occurred 500-1000 years before Esther was born, like Haman's deep hostility toward the Jews due to a tribal feud and the subsequent disobedience of a king (see Deuteronomy 25 and 1 Samuel 15). Only an omnipotent and omniscient God could bring together centuries of events and people to ultimately produce the preservation of His chosen nation. What could be seen as bad circumstances in Esther's life really were the divine hand of God working all things to His perfect good.

Esther was an orphan who was raised by her cousin Mordecai after her parents died. She lived in Susa under the rule of King Xerxes, like so many Jews that were taken from Jerusalem. During a celebration, King Xerxes became disgruntled with his queen when she would not appear before him. Queen Vashti was exiled and never allowed before the king again. In her absence, the king became lonely and desired a new queen. Virgins from the entire kingdom were brought to the palace, groomed, educated, and prepared for a meeting with the king. Of all these young ladies, Esther found favor in the king's eyes and was crowned queen.

There were no coincidences in these events. God's divine purpose can be seen in every seemingly insignificant circumstance. Historically, the Jews were taken into exile around 600 B.C. in the time of Daniel because of their continued disobedience to God's commands (see Daniel 1:1). We don't know the reason for her parent's death, but it was not untimely because it placed Esther in this specific location with her older cousin Mordecai, a descendant of the tribe of Benjamin. Esther was a young, beautiful woman at the perfect age for courting, but she was not yet married; therefore, she met the king's criteria. When she was taken into the palace and prepared for the king, her guardian, Hegai, the king's eunuch, found favor with Esther. "And the young woman pleased him and won his favor" (Esther 2:9). This should be no surprise since the Lord influences the lives of everyone, even those who are not of His chosen lineage. Esther found favor in the king's eyes, likely through Hegai's actions.

This love story does not end here. For the actual love story was not between King Xerxes and Queen Esther, but rather it was between the Creator and His chosen people. God's ultimate purpose was not just to raise up an orphaned Jewish girl to be queen. He also had a plan to use Esther to save the entire Jewish race from annihilation. After Mordecai refused to bow down and pay homage to Haman, one of the king's highest officials and, historically, an enemy of the Jews, "Haman sought to destroy all the Jews" (Esther 3:6). When Mordecai learned of this, he went to Esther and asked her to speak with the king. Though hesitant, for it was against the law to approach the king without being summoned, she did as Mordecai requested. Once again, she found favor with the king and was able to speak with him. When the king learned of Haman's deception, he immediately ordered that Haman be hung.

In what seemed like a time of great despair for the Jews, the Lord was with them and saved them. He directed each event and brought the outcome of His desire. Mordecai recognized the sovereignty of God when he explained to Esther, "Do not think to yourself that in the king's palace you will escape any more than all the other Jews. For if you keep silent at this time, relief and deliverance will rise for the

Jews from another place, but you and your father's house will perish. And who knows whether you have not come to the kingdom for such a time as this?" (Esther 4:13-14). Mordecai believed God would save His people, and Mordecai also recognized that the necessary steps for that rescue might possibly involve his young, naive cousin.

The love story of a Creator for His chosen people continues in your life. As Esther was placed in this particular circumstance for "such a time as this," so you have also been diagnosed with cancer for "such a time as this." The Lord has known you from before your birth. "Your eyes saw my unformed substance; in Your book were written, every one of them, the days that were formed for me, when as yet there was none of them" (Psalm 139:16). He has known you from eternity past to this particular moment in time. He has orchestrated each event of your life for His specific purpose. "I know, O Lord, that the way of man is not in himself, that it is not in man who walks to direct his steps" (Jeremiah 10:23). Even now, He continues to work through you, during your treatment, during the unexpected events of your cancer course, and for the duration of your life.

> As Esther was placed in this particular circumstance for "such a time as this," so you have also been diagnosed with cancer for "such a time as this."

Perhaps you are feeling upset or angry at this point. Perhaps you feel like a pawn in a chess game or a puppet on a string. Let me assure you that God may have providential control over your life, but you also have the ability to make decisions. Your choices have real outcomes and consequences. God's providence, and our ability to choose, work concurrently together. According to Wayne Grudem, "He (God) somehow upholds our ability to make willing, responsible choices, choices that have real and eternal results, and for which we are held accountable."[6]

In his book, *Chosen by God*, Dr. Sproul defines humans as free, meaning we have the ability to make decisions. Humans are free, but they are not autonomous. Humans do not have the ability of "self-rule" because we are subject to the One who has ultimate control. "It is not freedom that is canceled out by sovereignty; it is autonomy that cannot coexist with sovereignty."[7] King Xerxes made a real choice when he chose Esther to be his queen; "… the king loved Esther more than all the women, and she won grace and favor in his sight more than all the virgins" (Esther 2:17). Yes, Esther was queen because Xerxes chose her, but looking one step further, Esther was queen ultimately because God, through His divine sovereignty, ordained her to be queen.

Another way we can distinguish between our ability to make real decisions and God's guiding hand is to look at sin. Humans, in their fallen nature, will always choose sin unless God intervenes with grace. Apart from Christ, we can do nothing good. We will always choose to sin (Romans 7:17-19). God, however, cannot (and does not) cause us to sin. Whenever we choose to sin, we are acting outside the will of God, but our sovereign God can still use our sin for good. Remember the sin committed against Joseph by his brothers? Joseph was sold by his brothers into slavery, but God was able to use Joseph to save those same brothers—and his entire family—from the famine that occurred in Canaan many years later. Genesis 50:20 says, "As for you, you meant evil against me, but God meant it for good, to bring it about that many people should be kept alive, as they are today." Though God can use sin for His good, sin will also have consequences. David experienced this when his son died because of the sin he committed with Bathsheba. "Nevertheless, because by this deed you have utterly scorned the Lord, the child who is born to you shall die" (2 Samuel 12:14).

God's sovereignty can be a difficult subject to comprehend and accept, especially when considering a cancer diagnosis. To say that God ordained your cancer is a tough truth to swallow, but the Bible does give us clear examples of God's difficult providences. Job is a recognizable example of God's hard providence, as we are given a glimpse of the conversation God and Satan had regarding Job. God allowed Satan to inflict pain and suffering upon Job. Another example would be Christ on the cross. God ordained that Christ should suffer and die (Acts 2:23) so that we would have a rescuer. In our finite wisdom, humans can never fully understand the workings and will of God especially when His will includes hard providences. Paul reminds us in Romans that we are clay in the hands of a Potter—creations of someone wiser than us. "But who are you, O man, to answer back to God? Will what is molded say to its molder, 'Why have you made me like this?'" (Romans 9:20).

We may not understand His ways, but we can trust in His goodness and mercy. "For the word of the Lord is upright, and all His work is done in faithfulness...The king is not saved by his great army; a warrior is not delivered by his great strength...Our soul waits for the Lord; He is our help and our shield.

> We may not understand His ways, but we can trust in His goodness and mercy.

For our heart is glad in Him, because we trust in His holy name" (Psalm 33). God has ordered your life to reveal His own glory and accomplish His own will. He has allowed this cancer diagnosis to fall upon you for a reason, and you can trust Him to be faithful and to help you throughout the journey even if you do not understand His ways.

Can you trust God? Absolutely! In fact, not only can you trust God, but you can find peace in God's sovereignty. You can find relief from the fear, worry, and stress that plagues non-believers during a trial, and you can find hope in God's perfect plan. If God has planned and purposed for you to live with cancer, then there can be no other plan that is better or, ultimately, more rewarding for you. At the end of your cancer journey—whether the Lord has cured you or chooses to bring you into Glory, I hope that you will look back on the journey and see all the good from this trial. I hope you will see the Redeemer walking with you through each step and unexpected event.

Amy was diagnosed with stage III breast cancer at the age of 62. She received surgery, radiation, and chemotherapy in attempt to cure the cancer. After the treatment was completed, I asked Amy about her journey. Obviously, it was difficult and long. She naturally had moments of anxiety and worry at the thought of it recurring. Despite all the challenges, she told me she could see God in every step, walking beside her, giving her comfort and peace. I asked Amy, if she could, would she change anything about her cancer journey. She said, "I would not wish this disease upon anyone, but my relationship with the Lord has never been stronger, and looking back, I can now see His purpose."

# CHAPTER TWO

# FINDING ANSWERS
# THROUGH PRAYER

Two weeks after the surgery to remove the cancer in her left breast, a 59-year-old retired schoolteacher named Mary had her first appointment with our oncologist. After a complete history was taken and the physical exam was performed, the oncologist quickly explained the next steps in the quest for curing her stage II breast cancer. The surgical site required about four weeks to heal. Once the wound had healed sufficiently, she would require four months of chemotherapy. After completion of chemotherapy, she would require radiation to the surgical site for about six weeks. Mary felt overwhelmed at all the necessary steps required to cure her cancer, but it was worth it to her. She knew the next six months would be tough and certainly life-changing, but her physician told her that she had an 80%, or better, chance for survival.[8]

## THE RIGHT OPTION

At the first or second appointment, once all the necessary studies for staging have been completed, your oncologist will present you with several options regarding cancer treatment. The standard of care for any type of cancer is the treatment proven by research studies or clinical trials to result in the best outcome, the highest cure rate or—in the case of more advanced cancers—the treatment that controls the cancer for the longest period of time. The types of treatments available are chemotherapy, radiation, or surgery. Some cancer treatments require a combination of two of these treatment types, while others may require all three. In the case of chemotherapy, a standard regimen may include a single drug or a combination of several drugs.

Oncologists must take several things into consideration when offering treatment. First, they must decide the ultimate goal of the treatment. Most people presume the purpose of cancer treatment is to cure, but seeking a cure is not always a realistic goal. Advanced cancers often cannot be cured, and there are other important goals to consider, such as comfort or palliation. If cancer treatment can increase comfort, then the treatment will be considered successful, even if it does not result in a cure.

Once the goal of the cancer treatment has been determined, the oncologist must choose a good treatment for the cancer type. The treatment could be a single drug or a regimen consisting of multiple drugs. Sometimes chemotherapy agents can be used to treat a variety of cancer types, but each cancer type has a standard of care, or a list of agents that produce the best results. For example, one particular chemotherapy agent, called Docetaxel or Taxotere, can be used to treat lung cancer, breast cancer, and prostate cancer. Some-

## HOW OFTEN IS CHEMOTHERAPY GIVEN?

Chemotherapy is given in cycles. Most chemotherapy regimens call for a two-, three-, or four-week cycle. The cancer type, and the recommended regimen, will determine the number of cycles for treatment. Each cycle is then divided into days. For example, the most common colon cancer regimen used is a two-week cycle (14 days), where treatment is given on Day One and repeated in two weeks. Alternatively, a lung cancer regimen may require treatment on Day One and Day Eight, with the cycle repeating every 21 days.

When chemotherapy is given with the intention of curing the cancer, a set number of cycles are planned. A breast cancer regimen usually requires four or six cycles, each lasting three weeks. A colon cancer regimen usually requires twelve cycles, each lasting two weeks. When chemotherapy is given for control, instead of cure, as with stage IV cancers, then the number of cycles may vary. This type of chemotherapy is usually given until it no longer works or until the side effects become intolerable. A few chemotherapy agents have a maximum amount that can be given in a lifetime, so the agent will automatically be discontinued if that maximum amount is reached. Other chemotherapy agents are limited by the side effects they cause.

times this medication is used alone, as is the case with prostate cancer. Other times, the medication is used with other chemotherapy agents, as with breast cancer. The agent can also be used in different doses, given either weekly or every three weeks. Therefore, the oncologist must choose not only the appropriate drug, but also the appropriate dosages and time intervals for it to be given.

Choosing the drug and dosage is probably the easiest part of this process, but now the oncologist must pick a treatment appropriate for an individual's overall health. Some regimens have more side effects and are more challenging than others. An elderly patient with many health problems may require a more gentle treatment than a younger person in very good health. An individual's performance status is based on daily living and how much he is capable of doing without the assistance of another individual. For example, a person who works full time and is able to complete normal activities will have a performance status of 100%, while a person who is in a wheelchair and unable to drive or care for himself will have a performance status of 50%. This evaluation can make a difference in the type of chemotherapy an oncologist offers.

Finally, the oncologist must pick a treatment that an insurance company will pay for, or what is affordable to the patient. New medications are being discovered and tested every day, but they must be approved for a particular cancer type before an insurance company will pay for the administration of the drug. Some chemotherapy agents cost thousands of dollars, so insurance companies want to make sure the agent is declared by the Food and Drug Administration (FDA) as being successful in fighting cancer before they will pay for the treatment. Before any drug is allowed to be used in the United States, it must undergo rigorous clinical testing (clinical trials will be covered in chapter seven) and gain approval from the FDA. All insurance companies are different with regard to medications they will allow and how much they will pay. Therefore, it is almost impossible for a physician to know all of the rules for each individual. Using medications that are not yet approved by the FDA for a particular cancer type generally requires data or research to be presented to the insurance company, and this exploratory treatment is usually reserved for more advanced cancers.

Several cancer therapies now come in pill form, and there can be a difference in cost for a prescription medication versus an intravenous medication. Intravenous medications are covered by traditional medical benefits, but prescription drugs are covered by prescription benefits. Once again, all benefits will vary from one insurance company to another.

With these basic rules in mind, the oncologist will present what he/she believes to be the best treatment option. In Mary's case, she received all three types of treatment, which is quite common for a breast cancer diagnosis. Since cancer treatment depends on varying factors, it is difficult to give you specifics on your treatment options.

Allow me, instead, to give you a few more patient scenarios. Carrie, from Chapter 1, had an advanced-staged lung cancer, so surgery was not a good option for her. She was treated with both chemotherapy and radiation. In Chapter 3, you will meet Jim. He was diagnosed with stage III colon cancer. After surgical removal of the cancer, he was given chemotherapy. His particular cancer type did not require radiation. While all three modalities (surgery, chemotherapy, and radiation) may not be used for every cancer type, we will look at each one in more detail.

SURGERY

Surgery is probably the easiest treatment type to understand, since the cancer is removed via a surgical procedure, which often requires anesthesia. Two major criteria must be met for this option to be considered. First, the patient must be healthy enough for a surgical procedure. Anesthesia alone is a significant risk, and many people suffer from complications after surgery, especially the elderly and those with several health problems. The surgeon may require a pre-operative clearance by asking a specialty physician, such as a cardiologist or pulmonologist, to evaluate an individual's surgical risk. Surgery is only chosen for "good" surgical candidates.

The second criterion deals with the surgeon's goal for performing the surgery. Surgery is often limited to early-staged cancers or solitary tumors. The surgeon will have more success in curing an early-staged cancer by completely removing a solid tumor, rather than trying to remove a cancer that is located in multiple places. Later-staged cancers often require much more invasive surgeries, and they often result in cancer recurrence. Obviously, cancer recurrence is a poor outcome for the risk of the surgery. Later-staged cancers can be "debulked," which means the surgeon removes as much cancer as possible, as is the case with ovarian cancer. The main goal for debulking the cancer is to remove as much of the tumor as possible for improving symptoms such as pain and increasing the effectiveness of chemotherapy.

## RADIATION

Radiation therapy is the use of ionizing radioactive particles to kill, or shrink, cancer cells. "The aim of radiation therapy is to deliver a precisely measured dose of irradiation to a defined tumor volume with as minimal damage as possible to surrounding healthy tissue, resulting in eradication of the tumor, a high quality of life, and prolongation of survival at competitive cost."[9] In other words, radiation therapy is a very precise agent meant to be a local treatment, rather than a systemic, or "whole-body," treatment. Some normal cells can be affected, but the goal is to target the cancer cells with minimal damage to normal cells. Radiation can be used as a single

## HOW OFTEN IS RADIATION GIVEN?

Much like chemotherapy, the amount of radiation is based on the type of cancer you have and whether the goal of radiation is cure or comfort. Once the radiation oncologist calculates the total amount of radiation to a particular site, the treatment will be divided up into daily doses. The doses are usually given Monday through Friday—not typically on the weekends. The number of doses can vary from 15 to 60 treatments. The amount of time required for the radiation to be administered is quite short. More time is actually spent positioning for the radiation treatment.

treatment, in conjunction with chemotherapy, or in sequential order with surgery or chemotherapy. In early-staged cancer, radiation can be an important modality for curing the cancer. In late-staged cancer, the radiation can be used for palliation purposes, such as relieving pain.

Ionizing radiation works to kill cancer cells by damaging the DNA. After the DNA is disrupted, the cell is no longer capable of maintaining the normal processes to function. Thus, the cell will die. The time it takes for a cell to die could be hours or days. In some cases, the cell will make an effort to repair the damage (recall the discussion in Chapter 1 on DNA repair mechanisms). A successful repair will be unlikely, as the radiation is given in small doses over a period of several days to weeks. The same theory holds true for normal cells that are also attempting to repair. Ideally, the cancer cells will be destroyed, and the normal cells will be able to repair. Since the effects of radiation are cumulative, once an area has been given radiation, it is difficult to give more radiation to that same site.

The physician in charge of radiation therapy is called a radiation oncologist. Because different types of tissues can handle different amounts of radiation, the radiation oncologist must calculate the proper dosage for the individual and cancer type. Dosages are measured in the international system of units known as "gray" (or Gy), and the total dose is then divided into smaller amounts, which are given on a daily basis. Prior to receiving the radiation, the radiation oncologist develops a treatment plan to determine the exact place on the body to aim the radiation. The area may then be marked with either a temporary or permanent marking during a simulation so that the same location is targeted with each treatment.

CHEMOTHERAPY

Chemotherapy is the use of chemicals to destroy cancer cells. Unlike surgery and radiation, it is a systemic (or whole-body) therapy instead of a localized therapy. Chemotherapy disrupts cells that are dividing, or replicating, DNA by targeting the essential elements needed for replication. Cancer cells are constantly dividing and making copies of their DNA, but normal cells only divide when necessary: i.e., when they need more workers to perform a particular task, or when a cell is getting old. Theoretically, the cancer cells will

# WHAT MEDICATIONS DO I RECEIVE WHEN I GET CHEMOTHERAPY?

There are several medications that are given in conjunction with chemotherapy called "pre-meds." Pre-meds are given for two main reasons—to prevent nausea and vomiting and to prevent allergic reactions. Most chemotherapy agents are given in conjunction with an intravenous (IV) anti-nausea medication. If the chemotherapy is known to cause a lot of nausea, then two medications for nausea may be used. There are several new advances in anti-nausea medications that help patients stay on schedule and receive adequate amounts of chemotherapy. Common medications that are used to prevent an allergic reaction are Tylenol, Benadryl, and steroids. Some of these medications can be given in pill form, and others are intravenous. Certain chemotherapy agents require another non-chemotherapy agent to help them work better. Other chemotherapy agents require fluids (hydration) to help protect the kidneys. Ask your healthcare provider to give you a list of all the medications and their purpose in your treatment.

be affected by the chemotherapy, while normal cells are spared. However, some normal cells do divide more often, such as hair cells, cells that line the stomach, and blood cells. Unfortunately, this non-specific action of chemotherapy means some normal cells are also affected because chemotherapy does not distinguish between healthy cells and cancer cells. It simply attacks cells that are dividing. This mechanism of action can help explain some of the side effects associated with chemotherapy, which will be discussed in Chapter 4.

Chemotherapy is often required when the cancer is bigger and/or found in the lymph nodes. Chemotherapy is also used more frequently than surgery or radiation for late-staged cancers. In some cases, chemotherapy is used prior to surgery in an attempt to shrink the mass so the surgery will be easier. Chemotherapy can also be given in conjunction with radiation. In this case, the chemotherapy improves the lethal effects of the radiation to the cancer cells. Most often, the chemotherapy dose is adjusted to smaller amounts when receiving concurrent radiation.

"Targeted agents" are the newest type of medications being studied and share some similarities and differences with chemo-therapy. Instead of destroying all cells that are actively dividing, these agents are meant to target specific, and unique, features of cancer cells. There are still some side effects associated with these medications, but they are usually less severe and generally better tolerated than chemotherapy. Often, these targeted agents are used in more advanced-staged cancers because they are studied and approved in advanced cancers first. However, with continued improvements in cancer research, these agents may one day replace traditional chemotherapy.

For now, in the setting of breast, colon, and lung cancer, chemotherapy remains the mainstay for treatment. Targeted agents do exist for these cancer types and do play a role, but most often, the targeted agent will be used in conjunction with chemotherapy. In rarer cancers, like renal cell carcinoma (or kidney cancers), targeted agents have almost completely erased the use of chemotherapy. A surge of agents are now available for kidney cancer, and the research for targeted agents remains a top priority for all types of cancer.

ENCOURAGEMENT FROM THE WORD

*...Do not be anxious about anything, but in everything by prayer and supplication with thanksgiving let your requests be made known to God.* (Philippians 4:6)

In this chapter, we have looked at the different types of treatment and the importance of making well-informed decisions about the various treatments. Mary required all three treatment modalities for her breast cancer and, no doubt, it was a very challenging time in her life. The six-month treatment was life-altering for her. When I asked Mary what helped her through the trial, she said, "Communicating with my Great Physician."

You have probably met with many physicians during this time, but do you personally know the Great Physician? In Matthew 9:12-13, Jesus told the Pharisees that He came "not to call the righteous, but sinners" for only the sick are in need of a physician. In Luke 5:17-26, Christ demonstrated His power as the Great Physician when He not only healed the paralyzed man, but also forgave his sins. Perhaps you have communicated with many physicians during this time, but have you communicated with the Great Physician? Have you spoken to Him about your worries, concerns, fears, and future? Communicating with your Heavenly Father through prayer is essential, not only during times of trial, but through all circumstances of life.

Many books have been written on the subject of prayer covering

> Communicating with your Heavenly Father through prayer is essential, not only during times of trial, but through all circumstances of life.

the purpose, the proper way to pray, and the results of prayer.[10, 11] People used prayer throughout the Bible to communicate with God. Prayer was used to present requests to Him, to praise Him, or to simply be in fellowship with Him. The cancer journey will be much easier if you communicate with the Divine Healer (Psalm 103:3). Just like your oncologist will want to see you for regular visits to make sure you are doing well, your Great Physician also wants to meet with you regularly. Perhaps you think you don't have the time? Jesus found time for prayer during all of His teaching, preaching, and His miracle-performing. As Mark 1:35 describes, "And rising very early in the morning, while it was still dark, He departed and went out to a desolate place, and there He prayed." Perhaps you don't know how to pray, or has it been awhile since you last prayed? The Bible gives clear direction on how to pray because Jesus taught His disciples the proper place and method for praying in Matthew 6:5-13.

Prayer is more than just a one-sided conversation. Prayer also means asking for wisdom and direction from God through His Word. John 16:24 says, "...Ask, and you will receive, that your joy may be full." Sometimes, however, He may not give us the answer we want, and He may not grant all of our requests. The Bible shows the unfortunate consequences of sin and a sinful world for God's chosen people. It took 40 years of wandering in the wilderness before the Israelites were able to enter the Promised Land (see Numbers 14:26-34). So, how do we discern the right things to ask, and how do we wait patiently for Him to grant our petitions? How do we begin to understand His perfect ways? Let's look at the example of Christ praying in the Garden of Gethsemane.

Matthew 26:36-46 gives an account of Jesus in the garden before He was betrayed and arrested. Jesus, being both mortal man and the perfect Son of God, went to the garden with two pleas for His Heavenly Father. While, on the surface, these two pleas may seem quite opposite, they both actually illustrate the point and purpose of prayer. Christ first asked that the "cup" might pass from Him (Matthew 26:39). In other words, Christ asked God to remove the suffering that was about to happen. Let us not move past this point too quickly. The suffering that Christ was about to endure is something you and I cannot fathom. We may think that His suffering and death were of little consequence since He is God. The

Bible says that Christ was in "agony" and that "His sweat became like great drops of blood falling down to the ground" (Luke 22:44). E.M. Bounds describes the hours of Christ's betrayal, torture, and crucifixion as "…the weakness of all His weaknesses, the sorrow of all His sorrows, the agony of all His agonies."[12] Christ was the Chief Sufferer.

There is nothing wrong with presenting a request to God, as Christ requested that the "cup" might pass from Him. The Bible instructs us to pray. "Is anyone among you suffering? Let him pray" (James 5:13). Not only are we instructed to pray, but our prayers can be powerful. "The prayer of a righteous person has great power as it is working. Elijah was a man with a nature like ours, and he prayed fervently that it might not rain, and for three years and six months it did not rain on the earth. Then he prayed again, and heaven gave rain, and the earth bore its fruit" (James 5:16-18). Believers can petition God for certain outcomes and God hears our requests. When the Lord decided to destroy Sodom, He told Abraham His plan. Abraham asked God to save Sodom if just ten righteous men could be found (Genesis 18:22-33). Though ten righteous men could not be found and Sodom was still destroyed, the Lord heard the petition of Abraham on behalf of the righteous people dwelling in Sodom. In the end, the righteous were spared, but the city was not.

Though we are instructed to pray, our prayers are not necessarily capable of changing the set events of God's will. Besides Christ, there are many Bible characters who have petitioned God for the "cup" to pass. Paul asked for the thorn to be removed from his flesh (2 Corinthians 12:8). David "sought God on behalf of the child" (2 Samuel 12:16). David asked the Lord to heal his child—the child he had conceived with Bathsheba in an adulterous relationship. Despite their pleas, the Lord's will was not changed.

Notice Christ's second plea in the Garden—that God's will be done. Christ linked this request with the word "nevertheless" to show that His first request was subordinate to His second request. Christ submitted to the will of His Father. He became perfectly obedient to the Father's will. "Although He was a son, He learned obedience through what He suffered. And being made perfect, He became the source of eternal salvation to all who obey Him" (Hebrews 5:8-9).

We too should bring our requests to God, but we must also link our request with a "nevertheless." We must pray, more importantly, for the Lord's will to be done, and we must submit obediently to the cup that God has given us.

Why must we pray for the Lord's will to be done? Because God is omniscient (see 1 John 3:20 and Psalm 139); He has a viewpoint that is very different from ours. The Lord knows the beginning and the end of every circumstance and situation. If you have ever been to a football game, you can appreciate the varying vantage points of the field referee versus the referee located in the press box. The referee who sits in the press box has a very different view from the referee on the field. The field judge has a viewpoint that is limited to a particular situation in the present time, while the referee in the press box can see the entire play unfold and has the ability to watch the footage multiple times to make the proper call.

We will never fully understand the "big picture" in this life, and we can never grasp all the work God is doing. He sees our entire life and the lives of those around us. He knows the past, present, and future of all living beings. Just for a moment, suppose that God had allowed the cup to pass from Christ. It seems reasonable and logical that an innocent man should not die for the sins of others. The call of "innocent" from the field referee should be correct, but do you realize that this call would condemn us all to death? If there is no sacrifice for our sins—if there is no reconciliation with the Father through Christ—then we are a people without hope. Our Heavenly Father made the call based on His "big" picture. Christ became guilty so that we might be saved.

Praying for a cure is our first plea to God, but we must have a second plea that is actually more important than the first. Our second plea must be based on what will glorify God—how our lives will glorify Him. God may choose not to heal and cure cancer, just as He chose not to spare His Son from death. In this situation, we should take Bounds's advice, "We ought to submit patiently and tearfully, if need be, but sweetly and resignedly, without tremor, or doubt, to the cup pressed by a Father's hand to our lips."[12] The prayer of submission does not mean that we didn't pray hard enough. It does not mean we aren't one of God's favorites. It simply means that the cure was not part of His perfect will. Why? As we mentioned in Chapter 1, the only suitable answer to that tough question is in Romans 8:28: "And we know that for those who love God all things work together for good, for those who are called according to His purpose." Even the holiest man or the most well-studied theologian will not always be able to discern God's plan or know why some are healed from cancer and others are not. "His purpose" will be what brings Him the most glory.

From my experience with cancer patients, I have seen that there are some people who completely defy the statistics by being healed and others who seem to become a statistic when God chooses not to heal. God can use a time of crisis, like a cancer diagnosis, to do wonderful things, such as deepen your relationship with Him or bring another person into a relationship with Him through you. God used Paul and Silas in jail in Philippi to bring the Gospel to the jailer and his household. As a result, they believed in Christ (Acts 16:25-34). Paul's suffering was part of God's salvation plan for the jailer. Can God use your cancer to bring salvation to another? Make Christ's second plea your own—that God's will be done in your life.

> Make Christ's second plea your own—that God's will be done in your life.

Of course, you should pray for God to cure your cancer. Christ prayed three times for the cup of God's wrath to pass from Him while He was in the garden. He didn't do this because He thought God wasn't listening or couldn't hear Him. Rather, He was persistent. He made His request known to the Father over and over because it was grieving Him. God desires to hear our requests. Each time you receive test results or are due for another chemotherapy treatment, pray to God and present your requests to Him.

Don't stop praying. Pray for a cure. Pray for God's will. Pray without ceasing (1 Thessalonians 5:17). Pray for your day to day living—that you may be more like Christ. Pray that He would be all that you need. Keep praying; keep reading the Scriptures! You have a lot of work to do. Cancer is not a time for spiritual vacation. It's more like going into a spiritual battle. At the end of His prayer,

Christ rose and went to work doing His Father's will (Matthew 26:46). He didn't sit around anxious, depressed, worried, or fearful of the future. He didn't run away and hide under the covers of His bed. He knew tough times were ahead of Him, and He went into action. You also have work ahead of you that needs to be done. God has a plan and purpose for your journey through cancer. Get up and take care of business. In the face of opposition, remember the words in Isaiah 50:7, "But the Lord God helps me; therefore I have not been disgraced; therefore I have set my face like a flint, and I know that I shall not be put to shame."

Perhaps this scene in the garden is nothing like what you are experiencing. Perhaps you can only relate to the "human" side of what Christ experienced. After all, we are not capable of knowing when, and how, we will die. Christ knew His death was near. He knew of the pain and suffering that was to come. As humans, we can empathize with His emotions toward suffering and death. We are also likely in anguish about death because we fear it. If you read the scripture again, you should take note that, in none of the accounts of Jesus in the garden, do we find even a mention of fear. I encourage you to look to Christ, the man, for your example through this journey. Isaiah 41:10 commands you to "fear not, for I am with you; be not dismayed, for I am your God; I will strengthen you, I will help you, I will uphold you with My righteous right hand." For those who rest securely in Christ, death is not something to fear (Psalm 23:4), neither is pain or suffering. Part of your prayers should include asking God to remove your fears.

Despite the intense, blood-sweating feelings Christ had, He acknowledged that God's will should be done in the end. Submitting to the Father's will is the most important action to take during your journey. Recognize the ability and might of God. He is all-knowing, "For the foolishness of God is wiser than men, and the

> Submitting to the Father's will is the most important action to take during your journey.

weakness of God is stronger than men" (1 Corinthians 1:25). He is all-powerful, "Behold, I am the Lord, the God of all flesh. Is anything too hard for Me?" (Jeremiah 32:27). He is just, "A God of faithfulness and without iniquity, just and upright is He" (Deuteronomy 32:4). He is full of compassion and love for His flock. "Remember Your mercy, O Lord, and Your steadfast love, for they have been from of old" (Psalm 25:6). With all of these attributes, do you believe that He knows what is best for you?

Do you need to start praying? Still unsure of what to say? Here is an example. *Almighty God, I desire to know You as the Great Physician, for Your Word proclaims You as the Healer. I recognize and believe that You are capable of all things, even moving mountains, so I know You are able to cure me of cancer. I also know that You have a divine reason for why I must suffer with this disease and I want to fulfill Your purpose. I ask, Lord, that You would walk beside me during this trial and comfort me when I'm struggling. Please remove my fear. Throughout this journey, I ask that You guide and direct those who are caring for me. Please give wisdom to the doctors, nurses, and healthcare staff, and please give patience and understanding to my family and friends. Ultimately, Father, I pray for Your perfect will to be done in my life. Use me for Your glory. Thank You for loving me and saving me from my sins through Your Son, Jesus Christ. I ask all of these things in His name. Amen.*

# CHAPTER THREE

# FINDING GOD'S PROVISION

Jim and I were discussing the side effects he was having from the chemotherapy that was meant to cure his stage III colon cancer. He received chemotherapy every two weeks. By the tenth cycle, he was experiencing more fatigue and diarrhea. After we spent some time talking about things he could do to minimize the diarrhea, including foods to eat and medications to take, he pulled out a piece of paper from his pocket. "Now that we've discussed my cancer, could you please explain this bill to me?" he asked with a touch of anxiety. The paper causing him anxiety was not actually a bill, but a statement from his insurance company listing the money they had paid to our office called an "Explanation of Benefits," or an EOB. In addition to the office visits, nursing care, and lab work, several thousands of dollars in chemotherapy charges were listed. He was already nervous about the cancer and did not need another thing to worry about, especially not money.

## THE HEALTHCARE SYSTEM AND YOUR INSURANCE

Health insurance and the healthcare system in our country have become increasingly complicated. Many people are confused about how their health insurance operates in daily living and cannot comprehend how insurance functions during a significant illness like cancer. Many people pay too much money out-of-pocket because they do not know how to utilize their insurance appropriately. No one wants to discuss money during a health crisis; however, it is an important time to be aware of how health insurance works and the role of all involved parties. Understanding your insurance will also relieve some of the anxiety you may be feeling about finances. In this chapter, I would like to give you some basic information on health insurance to help you become more familiar with your insurance policy so that you can be an advocate for your finances. After all, your finances are your responsibility, regardless of who bills the insurance company. Before I give you examples of health insurance utilization in the common oncology practice, allow me to introduce a few standard definitions:

**claim** - A request for payment from the healthcare provider (or individual) to the insurance company under the terms of the policy.

**copayment** -The portion of a bill that you pay, usually at the time of service.

**deductible** -The amount you are required to pay toward healthcare services during a specified period, usually one year, before the insurance will begin to pay. This usually does not apply to office visits.

**HMO** - A medical plan in which members must use a specific network of providers.

**maximum out-of-pocket** – A limit on the amount you will pay out-of-pocket per year, which includes deductibles, coinsurance and co-payments.

**lifetime maximum** - The total amount of money your insurance will pay over your lifetime. If this amount is exceeded, then your insurance will no longer cover you.

**Medicaid -** A jointly funded federal and state program that provides hospital expense and medical expense coverage to the low-income population and certain aged and disabled individuals. For more information about Medicaid see their website at: http://www.medicaid.gov.

**Medicare -** A federal government hospital expense and medical expense insurance plan primarily for persons over age 65 and disabled persons. For more information about Medicare see their website at: http://www.medicare.gov.

**premium -** The payment (usually in monthly increments) for insurance coverage.

**primary care physician (PCP) -** A physician or other medical professional who serves as a group member's first contact with the healthcare system.

**prior authorization** - A requirement by the insurance company for physicians to declare the necessity of a procedure or drug before ordering.

**PPO** - A health insurance plan that offers discounted rates on services to members who use providers in the network. Often, if the individual seeks care outside the network, a smaller portion of the charges is reimbursed, and the patient's out-of-pocket expenses are higher.

**referral** - A request made by a physician for the patient to be sent to another physician. The primary care physician will usually give the cancer patient a referral to a specialist.

A DAY IN THE LIFE OF AN INSURANCE POLICY

Starting at the beginning of a cancer diagnosis and following the steps through the treatment process will give a clear picture of how a typical health insurance policy operates. Most patients are referred to an oncologist from another physician. HMOs require the primary care physician (PCP) to make all referrals, including referrals to oncologists, and the oncologist will be someone contracted with the HMO. Medicare and PPOs do not require a referral from the primary physician. Most PPOs do, however, have an in-network and out-of-network list of physicians. Benefits vary based on the chosen provider. Choosing an "in-network" over an "out-of-network" provider will decrease overall costs.

Prior to the first appointment with an oncologist, the office has likely already assessed your insurance and the benefits available.

Cancer treatment is very expensive, and the office must make sure they will be compensated for their services. It is important to remember that any physician's office is a business. Yet, unlike most fee-for-service businesses, a physician's office must purchase all their supplies, medications, and staff in advance. Then, after the service has been provided, the billing office will ask for reimbursement from the insurance company.

## I HAVE MEDICARE. DO I NEED A SECONDARY INSURANCE?

There are many different types of secondary insurances available. Some are specifically designed to work in conjunction with Medicare, but other general insurances can also be effective coverage. The purpose of secondary insurance is to cover the 20% that Medicare does not cover. Secondary insurances may have their own copayments, deductibles, and maximums, so you must read your policy very carefully and take into consideration all that has been covered in this chapter. One general rule about secondary insurances is that most will not cover anything that Medicare does not cover. It is rare for a secondary insurance to cover any cost where Medicare did not pay the first 80%. The secondary insurance does not provide you with extra services. It simply picks up the other 20% of the bill. It is standard practice for a physician's office to ask you to sign a document stating you will pay the 20% should the secondary insurance not cover it.

Cancer medications cost several thousands of dollars, and the staff needed to run the office must be trained to give these medications. If the office gives medications or services that are not reimbursed by the insurance company, then it will not be able to stay in business. Despite the need to be paid, a good office can manage the billing department well without sacrificing the importance of giving good care.

For each oncology visit, the receptionist may request a copayment, which is the designated amount of money set by your insurance company as partial payment for the office visit. The insurance company will then pay for the remainder of the visit. Each visit with a provider—whether a doctor, physician assistant, or nurse practitioner—will require payment of the copayment. However, most insurance policies do not require copayments for nurse visits or treatment visits.

During the first office visit, the physician should spend anywhere from 30 to 60 minutes asking questions about your medical history and completing a physical exam. The physician can then decide on a treatment plan, with perhaps some additional lab work and x-ray studies. Once the visit is complete, the physician will write a note based on his findings and recommendations. Then the doctor will bill the insurance company for the visit. This bill will be based on the complexity of the visit, how much time was spent on the case, and the diagnosis. After the initial visit, a "new patient" becomes an "established patient." Subsequent office visits should be shorter and much more direct, but the billing process will not change.

Tests, procedures, and treatments are all subject to the insurance deductible. A deductible is the amount of money the patient must pay before the insurance company begins to pay. Often, office visits are not subject to the deductible, and there are a few other exemptions. The amount of the deductible varies by insurance companies, but it usually ranges between $250 and $7000. Some insurance policies do not have a deductible, including a few HMOs, and Medicare has a deductible that can change from year to year. Deductibles are a yearly expense, usually restarting each January. This often makes the out-of-pocket expenses higher during the early part of the year and lower for the later part of the year. To maximize your savings, try to get any labs or x-rays done in November or December, so that they will apply to the current year's deductible.

Once the deductible has been achieved, the insurance will begin to pay. Depending on the policy, the amount the insurance will pay can vary and may only be a certain percentage. For example, the insurance may only cover 80% of lab, imaging, hospitalizations, or medications once the deductible has been met. This means the patient is responsible for the other 20% until the year is complete and the deductible is again required. Again, usually the office visit is paid at 100% by the insurance, regardless of the deductible. The only time a deductible, copayment, or percentage of payment will not apply is if the yearly out-of-pocket maximum has been achieved. When this happens, the patient will no longer have payments, and the insurance will pay all bills at 100% until the new year begins. When a cancer diagnosis is given, and the patient chooses to receive treatment, it is quite possible to reach the out-of-pocket maximum.

TESTS AND MORE TESTS

After the initial visit, and throughout the course of cancer treatment, the oncologist may need additional lab work or x-rays to determine the staging of the cancer and to see how well the cancer is responding to the treatments. HMOs have contracts with certain laboratory and imaging facilities and require members to use these facilities, or they will not pay for the test. The only exception would be in emergency situations or on weekends. Medicare and PPOs usually do not have a set location for testing, though certain facilities may not accept certain insurance plans.

Insurance companies may also decide how often labs and x-rays can be done. In the primary care setting, screening labs and tests can only be done once per year. For example, the PSA (prostate-specific antigen)—a screening test used to detect prostate cancer—and the Pap smear—a test used to detect cervical cancer—can only be performed once per year. Tests can be repeated if the result is abnormal. In the oncology setting, tests are done more often to evaluate the status of the cancer, but these tests are no longer declared as screening tests.

With certain insurance companies, a prior authorization may be required to obtain expensive tests like MRIs and PET scans. A prior authorization is a statement of medical necessity, provided by the ordering physician's office and addressed to the insurance company, which explains why the test or treatment has been ordered. It can take a few days for the prior authorization to be received, reviewed, and approved. In some cases, the physician or physician's representative may be required to speak with a member of the insurance team in what is called a peer-to-peer review. Once the review is complete, the insurance company will decide if the test or treatment is truly necessary. If the insurance agrees with the physician, the approval will be given, and the patient can have the treatment or test performed. If the insurance company denies the request, the ordering physician must decide whether to appeal the denial or choose an alternative, and often less costly, test or treatment.

## MEDICAL CODING

Medical coding is essential for payment. It is a confusing and constantly changing process that usually requires more staff than any other area of the medical office. Every diagnosis or problem has an associated number code from the International Statistical Classification of Diseases (ICD) book. Your provider must attach the correct diagnosis code to each office visit for the insurance company to pay. Labs, x-rays, and treatments must also have that same code attached to their bill for payment. Depending on the insurance guidelines, certain tests and medications may not be approved for certain diagnoses. This places limitations on what a physician can order. If a medication is not indicated for a particular diagnosis, then the associated code would be considered invalid upon billing. A physician will not want to order a treatment that the insurance company will deny payment for. Therefore, the physician must know the guidelines or must ask permission prior to treatment or testing.

## A SIMPLE EXAMPLE

Jim's story is an excellent example of all that has been discussed in this chapter. When Jim turned fifty, his primary care physician recommended a routine colonoscopy. The purpose of this procedure is to detect colon cancer, and it is usually performed by a gastroenterologist (a physician who specializes in the gastrointestinal tract). The gastroenterologist discovered a colon mass during the procedure and took a biopsy. The biopsy was sent to a pathologist (physician who evaluates tissue samples) to determine whether or not the mass was cancerous. When the mass was determined to be cancer, the patient was referred to a surgeon for removal of the mass. In a matter of days, the insurance was billed for the following:

(1)  A primary care office visit.

(2)  A consultation with a gastroenterologist.

(3)  A colonoscopy.

(4)  A pathologist to evaluate the tissue.

(5)  A consultation with the surgeon.

(6)  Surgery to remove the cancer.

As you can see, the costs add up quickly, and this is just the beginning. After the cancer was removed surgically, Jim met with our oncologist to discuss treatment. A CT scan was ordered for staging purposes, and a treatment plan was developed. The diagnosis code for colon cancer was placed in his chart for billing purposes.

## PRESCRIPTION BENEFITS

Angie was relieved when the oncologist did not recommend chemotherapy for her stage I breast cancer. After her surgery, he wanted her to take a pill every day for five years. Her only concern was how much the prescription medication would cost each month. She was on a fixed income and had several other medications to pay for.

Many oncology treatments and chemotherapy agents are made in pill form, and these are just as expensive as intravenous (IV) chemotherapy. However, oral medications utilize a different benefit from the insurance than traditional IV chemotherapy. Prescription benefits will vary by policy, and not all insurances offer prescription drug benefits, so it is important to know how the insurance handles prescriptions. For example, Medicare Part A covers hospital expenses, Medicare Part B covers office expenses, and Medicare Part D covers

## IS THERE ANY FINANCIAL ASSISTANCE AVAILABLE?

There are several financial assistance programs available, but taking advantage of them will require some effort. Some financial assistance programs will help with copayments and coinsurance, and others will help with prescription medication. Most pharmaceutical companies provide assistance for their products. Financial assistance may also vary based on the cancer diagnosis, and some agencies require proof of insurance denial or rejection letters from other agencies. Most financial assistance programs will consider income and may require a copy of your tax returns. Here are a few examples (and there are others) of financial assistance programs to get you started:

Patient Services Incorporated (PSI)
1-800-366-7741

The Patient Advocate Foundation
1-800-532-5274

Patient Advocate Foundation
Co-Pay Relief (PAF CPR)
1-866-512-3861

The Patient Access Network Foundation
1-866-316-7263

The Healthwell Foundation
1-800-675-8416

The Leukemia and Lymphoma
Society Patient Financial Aid
1-800-955-4572

Chronic Disease Fund
1-877-968-7233

prescription drugs. Unfortunately, many patients have Medicare Part B, but do not realize that their insurance does not cover prescription medications. Since we are discussing chemotherapy agents, allow me to mention the one exception to this rule. A small list of oral chemotherapy medications is covered by Medicare Part B if there is an equivalent IV form of the medication available.

A copayment is usually required for prescription medication, and that copayment can vary based on several different factors. First, the prescribing of name brand medications versus generic medications will change the copayment amount. When a pharmaceutical company develops a new drug, it receives a patent from the Food and Drug Administration (FDA), giving it exclusive rights to market that drug. After a certain number of years, the patent will expire, allowing other companies to make the drug and sell it in a generic version. Naturally, the original "name-brand" drug is more expensive than the generic because the market becomes flooded with generic medications once the patent expires.

Copayments for medication can also be affected by what is called the "tier system." Insurance companies contract with certain pharmaceutical companies to get better prices for medications. Drugs in lower tiers will be cheaper than drugs in higher tiers. Unfortunately, very few people have the entire list of drugs memorized, and very few physicians will attempt to memorize the list, so you are responsible for knowing which medications are on which tier.

The third factor in copayments will be the utilization of a mail-order pharmacy to get larger quantities of medication. Often, the copayment will be lowered if medications are given in three-month intervals through the mail-order pharmacy instead of using the local pharmacy on a monthly basis. However, the physician's office may not know which mail-order pharmacy your insurance utilizes. For example, Blue Cross/Blue Shield has many different plans available, and each plan may be contracted with a different mail-order pharmacy.

Finally, a prior authorization may be required for prescription medications. The insurance may deny the medication if the prior authorization has not been completed. Pharmacies may not be aware of the need for a prior authorization and will only receive a denial when trying to fill the prescription. If your insurance is denying a particular medication, then you should check to see if a prior authorization is needed. If so, then your physician will be able to fill out the prior authorization request.

The following is an example of how prescription benefits work. Angie was prescribed medication A to treat her breast cancer. Her monthly copayment was $50, and it was sometimes difficult for Angie to afford her medication. When she asked her pharmacist about the cost, he suggested that she try medication B. Medication B was similar to medication A, and it was an appropriate alternative for treating Angie's breast cancer. The pharmacist told Angie that medication B was now being made in a generic form.

Angie's oncologist had no problem switching her to the generic medication. This reduced her copayment to $20 per month. In addition to the generic drug being cheaper, Angie's insurance also had a contracted mail-order pharmacy and could fill the prescription for a three-month supply that would only cost Angie $40 instead of $60. The switch to a generic drug and the use of a mail-order pharmacy saved Angie $110 in a three-month period of time. Be aware that a pharmacist is not likely to mention the cost savings of a mail-order pharmacy because this will cost him your business. This example should encourage you to understand your prescription benefits and to be active in seeking an explanation of the benefits. Many people pay unreasonable prices for their prescription drugs because they do not understand their insurance plan.

## ENCOURAGEMENT FROM THE WORD

*Therefore I tell you, do not be anxious about your life, what you will eat or what you will drink, nor about your body, what you will put on. Is not life more than food, and the body more than clothing? Look at the birds of the air: they neither sow nor reap nor gather into barns, and yet your heavenly Father feeds them. Are you not of more value than they? ... But seek first the kingdom of God and His righteousness, and all these things will be added to you.* (Matthew 6:25-26, 33)

When considering finances and the healthcare system, it is easy to become anxious about the cost of cancer. Even the best health insurance may not be able to protect you from the debt brought on by treatment. The last thing Jim wanted to worry about was the cost of his cancer treatment. He had a mortgage to pay, one son in college, and another one who would be entering college a few years into the future. Was he about to spend all of his money fighting this disease? Would he lose all his retirement funds that he had worked so hard for? Cancer costs can cause us to lose sight of Who is in control and Who provides for our needs—both our spiritual needs and our physical needs.

The Bible identifies our Provider, and His name is "Jehovah-Jireh," the God who provides (Genesis 22:14). In Genesis 12, God chose Abraham (then called Abram) to be the father of many nations. He instructed Abraham to pack up his family and all his possessions and move to an unrevealed location. The Bible tells us, "And he went out, not knowing where he was going" (Hebrews 11:8). The journey to the promised land of Canaan was 1500 miles, and it included many stops along the way.[13]

Throughout the journey, from Genesis 12 to Genesis 22, the Bible clearly shows how the Lord provided for Abraham and his family. In Egypt, Abraham and his wife Sarai were protected from Pharaoh when she was taken into his home (Genesis 12). God provided Abraham with great wealth and many possessions (Genesis 13:2). The Lord provided a victory to Abraham when King Chedorlaomer's army took Lot, Abraham's nephew, captive (Genesis 14). God even provided a new name to Abraham to solidify His covenant, for Abraham means "father of a multitude" (Genesis 17:6-7). In his old age, God provided Abraham with a son to finally fulfill the promise He made to Abraham twenty-five years earlier (Genesis 21:5).

After proving Himself many times as a provider for all of Abraham's needs, the Lord again fulfilled His promise by providing a sacrifice. After Isaac was born, the Lord instructed Abraham to take Isaac to Mount Moriah and sacrifice him as an offering. This was a test to see if Abraham loved God's gift of Isaac more than he loved God Himself. Abraham did not argue or ask any questions, and he did not delay or make any excuses. "Abraham rose early in the morning, saddled his donkey, and took two of his young men with him, and his son Isaac. And he cut the wood for the burnt offering and arose and went to the place of which God had told him" (Genesis 22:3). Abraham simply obeyed.

Upon arrival to the designated site, Abraham built the altar to the Lord and placed his only son on that altar. As he proceeded to follow the Lord's instructions, an angel of the Lord stopped Abraham and told him not to harm the child. The Lord then provided a ram in the thickets as a substitute for the sacrifice. Abraham made the sacrifice and worshipped the Lord. As the Bible says, "So Abraham called the name of that place, 'The Lord will provide'; as it is said to this day, 'On the mount of the Lord it shall be provided'" (Genesis 22:14).

The Lord provided for Abraham both physically and spiritually, and we can rest assured that He will provide for us too. Matthew 6:25-33 describes the most basic physical needs that our Heavenly

> The Lord provided for Abraham both physically and spiritually, and we can rest assured that He will provide for us too.

Father meets. He is the ultimate provider for our food, drink, and clothing. More importantly, this passage commands us to not be anxious about these basic physical necessities because our sovereign Heavenly Father will provide exactly what we need when we need it. God cares for His people, and He has proven Himself over and over—not just in the life of Abraham, but in the lives of men and women throughout history.

In the Garden of Eden, after Adam and Eve sinned and became aware of their nakedness, the Lord, in His mercy provided clothing for them (Genesis 3:21). After the Israelites were delivered from the land of Egypt, the Lord provided food and water for them in the wilderness with manna from heaven (Exodus 16) and sweet water from bitter water (Exodus 15). The New Testament also gives us assurance in the Lord's provision when Christ taught His disciples to pray, "Give us this day our daily bread" (Matthew 6:11).

Basic needs like food and clothing are wonderful for the birds of the air and the flowers of the field, but we are reminded in Matthew 6:26 that we are more valuable than birds and flowers. Our God knows us intimately, and He can give us more than the basic necessities. He gives financial assistance in times of economic hardship, new friends during times of loneliness, and peace during the storms of life. He gives us rest when we are weary (see Matthew 11:28). When Christ sent His disciples out to minister, He instructed them to take nothing but a staff, a tunic, and a pair of sandals—no food, no money, and no possessions (Mark 6:7-13). Christ wanted to show the disciples that the Lord would provide—not only for their basic needs, but for everything they would need to do His work. Paul also reminds us that "God will supply every need of yours according to His riches in glory in Christ Jesus" (Philippians 4:19).

All of our needs have been met by the Lord—even the greatest need of all. Just as the Lord provided a sacrifice for Abraham, He has also provided the ultimate sacrifice for us. We have a Savior who has paid the penalty for our sins, removing the condemnation upon us, and allowing us access to and blessing from, God. The greatest provision God ever gave was His Son. Jesus Christ endured death on the cross to cover our sins so that we might gain eternal life and fellowship with the Father. As the Bible explains, "For our sake He [God, the Father] made Him [Christ] to be sin who knew no sin, so that in Him [Christ] we might become the righteousness of God" (2 Corinthians 5:21).

We needed Christ's sacrifice because, through Adam, sin entered the world, and now all mankind is condemned to death (Romans

5:12). There is no sacrifice we can make, and no work we can perform, to atone for our guilt. In His great mercy, God provided the only possible sacrifice through Christ so that we might be counted as righteous sons and daughters of God. "He [Christ] is the propitiation for our sins, and not for ours only but also for the sins of the whole world" (1 John 2:2). When Christ took our sins at the cross, He turned God's wrath away from us so that we might be reconciled back to God.

God's provision of a Savior is infinitely more valuable than His provision of the physical needs of this temporary life. We can now dwell with Him in eternity. What should our response be to His promise of provision? Jesus commands us in Matthew 6:33 to "seek first the kingdom of God and His righteousness, and all these things will be added to you." By seeking first His kingdom, we are declaring that every action, every expenditure, and every ounce of time we have on this earth will be for the glory of God. Time, money, gifts, and resources cannot be wasted on the frivolous. Paul described the former things as "rubbish" when compared to the "surpassing worth of knowing Christ Jesus" (Philippians 3:8).

Seeking the kingdom could mean spending time reading the Word while in the infusion room or praying with a fellow patient who is in need. Seeking the kingdom could mean talking with an unbelieving family member about God's grace and mercy.

The second part of Jesus' command is to seek righteousness. One way this is done is through faith, for we are told in Romans 3 that God's righteousness is manifested through those who believe in Jesus Christ. In Romans 4 we are reminded that "Abraham believed God, and it was counted to him as righteousness" (Romans 4:3). Abraham had faith when he obeyed God and became a sojourner in a foreign land. Abraham had faith when he placed Isaac on the altar as a sacrifice. He knew the Lord would provide even before the ram was caught in the thickets (Genesis 22:8).

According to Hebrews 11:1, the definition of faith is "the assurance of things hoped for, the conviction of things not seen." Interestingly, the Latin word for provide means "to see," yet faith is believing in something that cannot be seen. Our Lord will provide for our needs; in other words, our Lord will "see" to our needs, so we must trust in Him to do so. Charles Spurgeon, in his sermon on Jehovah-Jireh said, "If our difficulties multiply and increase so that our way seems completely blocked up, Jehovah will *see* to it that the road shall be cleared. The Lord will *see* us through in the way of holiness if we are only willing to be thorough in it, and dare to follow wheresoever He leads the way."[14] Seeing the Lord's provisions requires faith. Consider Christ's words, "...If you have faith like a grain of mustard seed, you will say to this mountain, 'Move from here to there,' and it will move, and nothing will be impossible for you" (Matthew 17:20). Even if your faith is hanging on by a thread, follow Him, and He will not only provide for the way, but He will also lead you along it.

Throughout your life, but especially during your cancer journey, when anxiety and worry over basic needs can be rampant, follow the example of Abraham and the teaching of Christ. Put away anxiety and allow faith and trust in the Lord to dominate your heart and mind. Allow trials to prove your faith in God, rather than your doubt in His promises. Ask, and eagerly wait, for His daily provision. It may not be in the form of healing or money, but be assured that the Lord will provide for exactly what

> Allow trials to prove your faith in God, rather than your doubt in His promises.

you need in His perfect time. Look to Christ for your salvation, and rejoice in your Jehovah-Jireh.

The following hymn of John Newton can be a good reminder for you:[15]

Though troubles assail
And dangers affright,
Though friends should all fail
And foes all unite;
Yet one thing secures us,
Whatever betide,
The scripture assures us,
The Lord will provide.

The birds without barn
Or storehouse are fed,
From them let us learn
To trust for our bread:
His saints, what is fitting,
Shall ne'er he denied,
So long as 'tis written,
The Lord will provide.

His call we obey
Like Abram of old,
Not knowing our way,
But faith makes us bold;
For though we are strangers
We have a good Guide,
And trust in all dangers,
The Lord will provide.

No strength of our own,
Or goodness we claim,
Yet since we have known
The Savior's great name;
In this our strong tower
For safety we hide,
The Lord is our power,
The Lord will provide.

When life sinks apace
And death is in view,
This word of His grace
Shall comfort us through:
No fearing or doubting
With Christ on our side,
We hope to die shouting,
The Lord will provide.

CHAPTER FOUR

# FINDING PEACE
# DURING THE BATTLE

One week after her first dose of chemotherapy, Barbara was scheduled to see me to make sure she had tolerated the treatment well. She reported the side effects she experienced—some nausea starting three days after treatment, a little bit of appetite loss, but—thankfully—no vomiting. After our conversation, she admitted, "It wasn't as bad as I thought it would be." Then she asked one of the usual questions I receive during a visit like this, "When will I lose my hair?" She was already making plans to pick out a wig. She left the appointment with some additional information regarding her chemotherapy and how best to deal with the side effects.

## The Most Frequent Questions

The two most frequent questions new cancer patients have are, "Am I going to be sick all the time?" and "Will I lose my hair?" Not surprisingly, a new patient's first questions usually have nothing to do with the specifics of how the cancer was caused (go back to Chapter 1, if you skipped ahead). That comes later, once the first treatment is complete and the side effects are being managed. The first questions usually have nothing to do with money (see Chapter 3). That comes at the end, when you survey the large amount of money spent for treatment.

Instead, the first questions are usually about the side effects of chemotherapy and radiation. There is a lot of fear associated with chemotherapy and radiation because these medications are toxic to the body. Despite their side effects, the treatments are effective at curing, or controlling, cancer. The goal of treatment is to provide the proper amount of chemotherapy or radiation without intolerable or unmanageable side effects. This chapter will help patients deal with their treatment by addressing the top side effects associated with chemotherapy and radiation.

## Top Side Effects from Cancer Treatment
## Nausea and Vomiting

One of the most satisfying things about my job is helping those who are suffering from chemotherapy side effects. When a patient walks into our office with nausea or vomiting, I want to get them relief immediately. I also want to prevent the nausea from reoccurring with the next treatment. Mr. Andrews had esophageal cancer. He was receiving both chemotherapy and radiation together, which is one of the toughest regimens an oncologist can prescribe. After the first cycle of chemotherapy, he came to our office severely dehydrated from vomiting. After a few hours of intravenous fluids and nausea medication, he left our office with a feeling of relief. I instructed him to come back each day for more medication and fluids. I told him we would work every day to make him more comfortable and to make this treatment bearable. Fortunately, he was able to finish all of his treatment.

## WHY AM I NAUSEATED RIGHT BEFORE I RECEIVE MY CHEMOTHERAPY?

Anticipatory nausea is a common condition where seeing the infusion room or office, or simply thinking of chemotherapy can cause nausea. The best way to treat anticipatory nausea is to take an anti-nausea medication before the appointment. The most commonly used medication for anticipatory nausea is Ativan (lorazepam).

Nausea is the unpleasant, often "wavelike," experience or urge to vomit that is associated with sweating, paleness, and weakness. Vomiting is the act of expelling contents from the stomach and small bowel through the mouth. Each is a phenomenon that may occur together or separately. Not all nausea will lead to vomiting, and not every patient will experience nausea prior to vomiting. Many things cause nausea and vomiting, including medications like chemotherapy or prescription pain medications, severe pain, abdominal disorders, infections, fear/anxiety, and distasteful smells. The cancer itself can cause nausea or vomiting, depending on where the cancer is located in the body. Radiation can also cause nausea or vomiting, depending on the site in the body that is receiving radiation such as the liver, abdominal region, or brain.

Chemotherapy-induced nausea and vomiting is a complex process that involves the stomach, small intestine, and the brain. There are several ways to prevent, or treat, nausea and vomiting, and new advances in pharmaceutical technology make nausea and vomiting more manageable. Patients are able to stay on schedule with their chemotherapy regimen and have a better response to the treatment by targeting the different pathways and causes of nausea with various pharmaceutical agents.

The first, and best, way to manage nausea or vomiting is to prevent it from occurring. Chemotherapy agents are classified based on how much nausea or vomiting they cause (see Appendix B). Those agents listed in the high category generally require two or three different ways to manage nausea or vomiting. The first medication is often given intravenously prior to chemotherapy and will help prevent nausea in the first twenty-four to forty-eight hours. In addition to the IV treatment, patients will also need at least one prescription (pill-form) medication to take at home. The chemotherapy agents in the low or minimal category may only require one medication, and they often do not require any management at all. Nausea related to radiation can be managed in much the same way as chemotherapy. Taking medication for nausea about thirty minutes prior to radiation treatment often prevents the nausea from occurring.

There are several simple, non-pharmaceutical techniques to prevent, or treat, nausea. First, eat small, bland snacks throughout the day. Large meals cause the stomach to stretch and may make nausea worse. Crackers, for example, are a great snack. Avoid highly acidic foods such as tomatoes and orange juice, which have a tendency to irritate the stomach lining. Next, keep cool. Avoid being outdoors if it is very warm and take care not to overexert yourself or exercise excessively. Drink plenty of fluids, but in small increments. Finally, smells can often trigger nausea, so try to avoid places or foods that cause an aversion to your senses. Mint candy can be beneficial for those who are sensitive to smell.

There are also alternative therapies used to manage nausea and vomiting. This includes acupuncture, aromatherapy, and herbal supplements like ginger. These agents are not FDA approved, so ask your physician prior to trying them. We will talk more about alternative treatments in Chapter 7.

ALOPECIA (HAIR LOSS)

Unlike nausea, hair loss cannot be prevented or managed with a prescription medication. Not all chemotherapy agents cause hair loss, but if your hair is going to fall out, then there is little you can do to stop it. There are, however, some things you can do to lessen the trauma of losing your hair. When I told Barbara that her hair would start thinning after the first cycle of chemotherapy and would likely be completely gone after the second, she decided to go to her local wig shop and pick out a wig before she lost it all. She wanted to find a wig that closely resembled her natural hair, and she knew that would be easier if she still had her hair for comparison. After finding the perfect wig, she asked her hairdresser to shorten her hair so she wouldn't have to see the large clumps of hair in the sink when it started to fall out. Naturally, Barbara didn't want to lose her hair, but she kept her attitude positive. She knew the hair loss was only temporary, and that it was for a good cause.

Theoretically, hair loss can be prevented if the chemotherapy does not reach the hair follicles. This theory has been known for years, but it is difficult to achieve. One technique includes immersing the hair in ice water during the chemotherapy delivery, but, as you can imagine, this is quite cumbersome. However, recently, several new products have been developed with the same technique and are more tolerable. The most common products are gel caps that provide cooling to the hair follicles. The efficacy of these products are somewhat mixed and most women will say they still lose hair.

## NEUROPATHY (NERVE DAMAGE)

Remember Jim with colon cancer from Chapter 3? His particular chemotherapy regimen included a drug called Oxaliplatin. One of the major side effects of this drug is neuropathy. Neuropathy is damage to the nervous tissue, which most often affects the hands and feet, causing them to feel numb, heavy, or to have a tingling sensation. There are several chemotherapy agents that can affect the nerve cells and some agents are toxic to nerves, but the exact mechanism for how chemotherapy damages the nerves is not completely understood.

Nerves are responsible for transmitting information to the brain and interpreting messages from the brain. There are two categories of nervous tissue—the central nervous system, which includes the brain and spinal cord and the peripheral nervous system, which includes all the nerves required to transmit or receive information from the central nervous system. To understand nerve function, consider what happens when you burn your hand on a hot stove.

Any movement of the hand toward a pot sitting on the stove requires the brain to send a signal to the spinal cord to utilize a motor nerve to move the hand. By mistake, instead of stirring the pot, your hand touches the stove burner. Once your hand senses the heat, a sensory nerve will transmit a signal back to the brain, telling you that heat is painful. Pain is a protective mechanism for the body to prevent tissue damage. Your brain then initiates a movement to stop the pain to minimize the damage to the hand. This movement will again be performed by the motor nerves.

Unlike nausea, which usually stops within a few days after treatment, nerves can take longer to heal. In extreme cases, nerves may never fully recover once they have been damaged. The best remedy for neuropathy is to stop the offending agent, which usually means stopping the chemotherapy. You can also ask your doctor about taking a B-complex vitamin or alpha lipoic acid, both of

## WHAT IS "CHEMO BRAIN"?

"Chemo brain" is a phrase used by patients to refer to the decrease in cognition and memory recall during, or after, chemotherapy. Most patients describe it as "being in a state of fog." Though widely used, you will not likely find this term in a textbook. It is difficult to characterize "chemo brain" because most chemotherapy agents do not cross the blood-brain barrier. The blood-brain barrier is the separation between the body's circulatory system and the cerebral spinal fluid that protects the central nervous system. Only certain molecules are allowed to cross into the central nervous system, and there are many factors that are dependent on that selectivity. Chemo brain is difficult to diagnose and manage because it is not well understood.

which are essential for nerve development and may aid in nerve repair. Be aware, however, that these supplements will not be able to reverse significant nerve damage.

If the nerve damage causes pain, and the pain persists after the treatment has stopped, there are some pharmaceutical remedies that can help manage the pain. The two most common groups of medications for nerve pain are anti-depressants and anti-seizure medications. Both of these classes of medications will have side effects, so it is important to ask your doctor to explain those that are most common. These medications are not typically used for numbness, but they are used for painful types of neuropathy.

DIARRHEA

Diarrhea is an increase in frequency of stools or a change in consistency to soft or watery stools. Patients suffering from diarrhea also complain of abdominal cramping and pain. This pain is usually relieved once the stool has passed. Diarrhea is potentially dangerous because it can result in a large loss of water, which can lead to dehydration. The main purpose of the large intestine is to reabsorb water from the stool back into the body. If the stool is passing through the large intestine too quickly, then very little water will be reabsorbed.

Many things can cause diarrhea, including diet, medications, infection, bowel surgery, irritable bowel disease, or inflammatory bowel disease. Diarrhea can result from eating excessive amounts of fiber or fruits, or from consuming milk products when lactose intolerant. Even high calorie/protein shakes such as Boost or Ensure can cause diarrhea in certain people. Laxatives can cause diarrhea if not taken as directed.

Chemotherapy agents can also lead to diarrhea. The three most common are capecitabine (Xeloda), 5-FU (fluorouracil), and irinotecan (CPT-11). These medications are commonly used in the treatment of colon cancer, but they can also be used to treat breast, lung or esophageal cancer. Patients receiving one of these agents may be given additional instructions on how to prevent, or manage, diarrhea if it becomes problematic. A dose reduction, or delay, in treatment may be required for moderate to severe diarrhea (more than five watery stools per day or diarrhea at night).

Diarrhea usually requires pharmacological management, but there are a few dietary measures worth trying. For mild to moderate diarrhea, make sure the diet is bland, and avoid excessive acid or milk products. Try eating more constipating foods like cheese and bananas. Also, try eating small meals, but continue to drink plenty of water. Stop taking medications that cause diarrhea, such as laxatives or stool softeners. Products that add fiber to the diet like Metamucil, may also cause diarrhea and should be used with caution.

Diarrhea that is excessively watery or occurring more than four to five times per day usually requires medication to slow down the bowel. An effective over-the-counter medication is called Imodium (loperamide), which works by slowing the normal movement of the intestines so that the stool stays in the colon longer, allowing more water to be reabsorbed back into the body. There are also some prescription medications that can be used to help with diarrhea, such as Lomotil. Finally, there are some injectable medications that can be used, but these are often only for severe cases of diarrhea.

Because of the large volume of water lost, moderate to severe diarrhea can result in dehydration and electrolyte imbalance. Notify your doctor immediately if you experience more than three to five stools per day or if you are having diarrhea at night. Dehydration from diarrhea can be severe enough to require hospitalization and can result in death if left untreated. If you are hospitalized as a result of dehydration, then medications will be given to treat the diarrhea, and IV fluids will be given for rehydration.

## Constipation

Constipation is the decrease in the number of stools in a given period of time or the hardening of stools. While some people think they must have a bowel movement each day, the number of bowel movements an individual has can vary from several bowel movements per day to one bowel movement every two to three days. This is why constipation is defined as a decrease from "normal habits."

The most common causes of constipation in the United States are a low fiber diet, inadequate fluid intake, or poor physical activity.[16] For cancer patients, constipation may also be caused by medications, chemotherapy, intestinal problems, or neuropathy. Some chemotherapy agents list constipation as a major side effect. Other common medications used in the oncology setting that can cause constipation include anti-nausea agents and pain medications.

Dietary changes are probably the easiest and safest way to relieve constipation. Drinking plenty of fluids is very important for moving the bowels. The purpose of the large colon is to reabsorb water from digested food and return the water back to the body. Staying hydrated will help prevent constipation. Increasing fiber in your diet to 20-25 grams per day will also relieve constipation. If this cannot be done with fruits, vegetables, and other high fiber sources, then a fiber supplement can be added, such as Metamucil, Benefiber, etc. Finally, thirty minutes of exercise per day will help the body better regulate the bowels.

While diarrhea is primarily managed by one or two pharmaceutical agents, there are several pharmaceutical agents available to manage constipation, and they each work in different ways. Stool softeners, such as Colace, are agents that force water to stay in the fecal mass instead of absorbing back through the large intestine. These agents are used to prevent constipation and to help pass hard stool. For example, anti-nausea medications given with the chemotherapy will often cause constipation, so some patients will take stool softeners 24 hours prior to receiving treatment to prevent constipation from occurring. Once constipation has begun, it is quite difficult to manage it with just stool softeners. Laxatives are a good agent to use in conjunction with stool softeners, but they should be used with care and should not be used for prolonged periods of time.

There are several different types of laxatives. Osmotic laxatives (e.g. magnesium citrate, milk of magnesia, Miralax) cause water to be collected in the bowel rather than to be reabsorbed. These agents work quickly to increase the speed of the stool through the intestines, and this can sometimes cause cramping. The stimulant laxatives (e.g. Senokot) increase the motor activity of the intestines causing the stool to move faster. These medications do not work as quickly as osmotic laxatives. Finally, lubricant laxatives (e.g. mineral oil) work much like stool softeners to soften the stool by lubricating the intestines.

Enemas and suppositories are another category of constipation medications, but they are only recommended in certain circumstances. Care should be taken when inserting anything in the anal area, especially during times of chemotherapy when the white cells and platelets may be low. These medications should only be used when a physician instructs you to do so.

FATIGUE (LOSS OF ENERGY)

After the third cycle of chemotherapy, Barbara was in our office for her routine checkup. She was wearing the stylish wig she had picked out. Her weight was stable, which told us that she was doing well with her appetite, and she admitted to managing the nausea quite well with the prescription medication. Her biggest complaint at this appointment was fatigue. She was feeling completely "wiped out." She would take a long nap in the daytime and still sleep for ten hours at night. She didn't have the energy to do her usual activities, like her morning walk and her errands to the grocery store. She wanted to know if she would ever get her energy back.

The most common side effect of chemotherapy or radiation is fatigue. Fatigue is the loss of energy, or the inability to do regular activities due to excessive tiredness. Fatigue is subjective. It is difficult to quantify, and it is difficult to determine its exact cause. Besides chemotherapy, other common causes include poor nutrition, lack of exercise, poor sleep, depression, anemia (low red blood cell count), low thyroid hormone, and side effects from medication. There are several tests and labs that can be used to diagnose, or rule out, certain factors that may be causing the fatigue.

Fatigue due to chemotherapy often falls into several categories. First, the medication itself can cause fatigue. Second, fatigue may result if the chemotherapy causes anemia, a condition of low red blood cells, which can be easily diagnosed with a blood test. Third, if the chemotherapy causes nausea or loss of appetite, then fatigue may be related to dehydration or poor nutrition. The body cannot complete normal activities if it does not have the nutrients to feed the cells.

## WHY DO I HAVE TROUBLE SLEEPING AFTER MY CHEMOTHERAPY?

As previously discussed, most chemotherapy infusions require pre-medications, and one of these medications is an intravenous steroid. The purpose of the steroid is to prevent an allergic response to the chemotherapy and help with nausea. In some cases, steroids may also be given by mouth the day before the treatment and the day after. Insomnia is one of the side effects of steroids, since most steroids tend to cause anxiety, jitteriness, and sleeplessness. One way to help prevent insomnia from steroids is to schedule the treatment early in the morning. The steroids will take effect throughout the day, but hopefully will not interfere with sleep. Other tips for insomnia include eliminating daytime naps and minimizing stimulating activities like watching television at bedtime. Sleeping pills should be used with caution. They can become addictive in certain populations, and they do not help with all forms of insomnia. However, when the cause of insomnia is related to medications like steroids, then a sleeping pill may be effective. The most common side effects associated with sleeping pills are headaches, drowsiness, and the feeling of being "drugged."

Of all the side effects of chemotherapy, fatigue may be the most frustrating, especially for people who are very active. Though it may seem counter-intuitive, the best way to combat fatigue is to stay active. Your body does need additional rest during this time, so take care not to overexert yourself. However, you should attempt to prevent weakening muscles. Simple exercises not only help fight fatigue, but they also help with depression and insomnia. For example, try walking outside to the mailbox and back. You can also do some things in your home, such as leg lifts from your chair or arm curls with some small hand weights. Another way to combat fatigue is to eat a well-balanced diet, which is covered in more detail in Chapter 8.

Finally, there are a few medications available to help with fatigue. These medications are traditionally used for hyperactivity or narcolepsy, but they can also effectively treat fatigue. However, since these medications are not specifically intended to treat fatigue, your insurance may not pay for them.

## MUCOSITIS (MOUTH SORES)

Mucositis is damage to the tissues of the mouth, including the tongue and inner wall of the cheeks, resulting in the formation of sores or ulcers. Certain chemotherapy agents and high doses of radiation to the mouth or neck can lead to mucositis, and mucositis can range from a slight irritation in the mouth to the inability to eat or swallow properly. Patients who smoke or have poor oral hygiene will have an increased risk for developing mucositis.

There is no cure for mouth sores so, once formed, they must heal on their own. The only way to stop the sores or ulcers from becoming worse is to delay, or discontinue, treatment. Some simple measures for managing the soreness are to keep the mouth clean by drinking plenty of fluids and utilizing salt water rinses or baking soda rinses. It is also important to use alcohol-free toothpaste and mouthwash because alcohol-based products can dry the mouth. If the mouth sores begin to affect your ability to eat and drink properly, then you may need IV fluids to keep you hydrated and liquid pain medication or numbing medication. Severe cases of mucositis may even require hospitalization.

There are a few prescription medications approved by the FDA for the prevention of mucositis. These medications are relatively new and can be expensive, but they may be necessary if you are developing mild to moderate mucositis. There are also a few medications to help soothe the symptoms of mucositis once it has started. The most common medication prescribed is a compounded drug with liquid Benadryl, Maalox, Lidocaine, and Nystatin. The specifics of this formulation can vary from office to office. Again, the medication will not heal the ulcer. It is simply a tool used for symptom relief.

Patients with head or neck cancer that require radiation to the mouth or tongue have a high risk for developing severe oral mucositis. Generally the radiation treatment lasts for six weeks, which is too long to endure inadequate oral intake or fluid intake. Your doctor may advise you to have a feeding tube placed so you can take in nourishment and fluids through a tube placed into your stomach. The placement of the tube is a minor surgery and can be done as an outpatient procedure. The biggest risk with having the tube placed is infection, but your doctor should show you how to adequately care for the tube or refer you to a nurse for care of the tube. The tube can easily be removed once the treatment is complete and you are capable of eating on your own.

LOW BLOOD COUNTS

A low blood count is a side effect from chemotherapy and radiation that you may not feel, but it is still important to talk about. Your physician will measure your blood counts frequently, so it is important for you to understand what the blood counts are. The Complete Blood Count (CBC) is a lab test that will be performed regularly by your doctor, and there are three quantities that will be evaluated—the white blood cells (WBCs), the red blood cells (RBCs), and the platelets.

The WBCs are the infection fighters of the body, and they are made in the bone marrow, which is found in the large bones, like the pelvis and sternum. Once the bone marrow makes a WBC, the cell circulates in the body for about 14-20 days. When bacteria or viruses enter the body, the WBCs work to fight the infection, which means the bone marrow may be required to produce more WBCs to perform the job adequately. For this reason, the WBCs often become elevated when there is an infection in the body. Chemotherapy will cause the white blood cell count to drop and, in some cases, radiation will also cause a drop if the radiation is near the bone marrow production sites. The lowest point in the blood cells after chemotherapy is called the "nadir." You are more susceptible to infection at the nadir because the white blood cells are at their lowest level and, therefore, cannot fight infection properly.

The RBCs are also produced in the bone marrow, and these cells typically live for 120 days once produced. The purpose of the RBC is to carry oxygen to all the tissues in the body. RBCs move through the lungs, pick up the oxygen, and are then pumped by the heart through arteries to deliver the oxygen. Once the oxygen is delivered to the tissues, then the RBCs return to the lungs through the veins to collect more oxygen. The condition associated with low RBCs is called anemia.

There are many causes of anemia, and chemotherapy is one of them. Chemotherapy will destroy the red and white blood cells alike. If necessary, the fastest way to replace RBCs is by a blood transfusion, which is a procedure where the individual is given a compatible do-nor's blood. Many people are concerned about the safety of the blood supply and the likelihood of disease transmission, such as HIV. However, this risk is quite low. According to the National Heart Lung and Blood Institute, the risk of developing HIV from a blood transfusion is one in two million.[17] If you are concerned, then you may be interested in a designated family donor. Contact your local blood bank for more information regarding family donation.

Platelets are the third cell type produced by the bone marrow, and they live for only a few days. Platelets result from the breakdown of a large cell called a megakaryocyte and are part of the clotting system of the body. When you cut yourself, or develop an injury, the platelets seal the cut and stop the bleeding. Chemotherapy will destroy the megakaryocytes and cause the platelets to become low, which will make you prone to bleeding and bruising. The fastest way to replace platelets is by a transfusion, similar to what we discussed with RBCs.

## WHAT PRECAUTIONS SHOULD I TAKE WHEN HAVING SEXUAL INTERCOURSE DURING CHEMOTHERAPY?

When receiving chemotherapy, it is very important to protect against conception. As discussed in Chapter 2, chemotherapy interrupts the replication, or production, of DNA through a variety of mechanisms. This can be detrimental to a developing baby and can cause birth defects or death. Therefore, some form of protection should be used and discussed with your physician prior to the chemotherapy administration. In certain cases, a pregnancy test may be required before chemotherapy will be given.

All chemotherapy agents are toxic to the blood cells, but some agents are worse than others. In general, a well-balanced diet full of vitamins and minerals like folic acid and iron will be beneficial to all cells, especially the red cells. Low blood cells will cause a delay in chemotherapy delivery, as most oncology practices require a certain number of white blood cells, red blood cells and platelets to be available before chemotherapy can be given safely. There are several pharmaceutical medications, called colony stimulating factors, available to aid the body in creating more of these blood cells. Prior to the invention of the medications, chemotherapy often had to be delayed or reduced in dose to be given safely. With these medications, patients are able to stay on schedule and receive the proper amount of treatment. Ask your doctor to explain the risks and benefits of these medications.

## ENCOURAGEMENT FROM THE WORD

*I cry out to God Most High, to God who fulfills His purpose for me.* (Psalm 57:2)

In most cancer clinics, there are many tears. Some are tears of sorrow and sadness, while others are of pain and suffering. There are tears of fear, tears of sin, and tears of regret. I remember the tears of Emily when she found out her small cell lung cancer had progressed. She knew it was time to tell her aging mother and didn't quite know how.

There are also tears of joy and thanksgiving. Marsha had the same diagnosis of small cell lung cancer, but her cancer was shrinking. She cried tears of joy at the good news and couldn't wait to call her daughter, who was away at college. With all of these tears spilled, the vast majority are probably spilled at home—with a spouse, a daughter or son, or with a friend. Many tears are spilled alone when no one is looking. You may be able to say, along with the Psalmist, "I am weary with my moaning; every night I flood my bed with tears; I drench my couch with my weeping. My eye wastes away because of grief; it grows weak because of all my foes" (Psalm 6:6-7). Yes, even men are allowed to shed tears, as David did in Psalm 6. Your loved ones will shed tears with you and for you. Your church family will shed tears. Your nurses and healthcare workers may even shed some tears. I have spilled tears with many of my patients, and I spill tears alone when I pray for specific patient needs.

There is nothing wrong with shedding tears. In fact, there are a few references of Jesus crying in the New Testament. In Luke 19:41-42, He wept for the city of Jerusalem right before he drove the peddlers out of the temple. In John 11:35, Jesus wept after the death of His friend Lazarus. In this particular circumstance, we may wonder why Jesus cried. He already knew of Lazarus's death before arriving in Bethany. Christ already knew the wondrous act He would perform for the sake of the "glory of God" (John 11:40). In fact, Christ deliberately delayed in going to the ill Lazarus when Mary and Martha sent word to Him.

Christ waited to go to Lazarus because He wanted to reveal God's glory to this family, His disciples, and the other Jewish mourners. Why, then, would Jesus cry if he already knew the outcome? Because, though Jesus was fully God, He was also a man. At the sight of Mary crying over the death of her brother Lazarus, Jesus was "deeply moved in His spirit and greatly troubled" (John 11:33). Jesus wept because He recognized the pain and sorrow that sin and death caused those whom He loved.

No matter how many tears you shed, you will never be alone if you are a child of the Father. God is with you, much like He was with David, "...the Lord has heard the sound of my weeping" (Psalm 6:8). Charles Spurgeon called tears "liquid prayers" and further wrote, "My God, I will weep when I cannot plead, for thou hearest the voice of my weeping."[18] The Lord hears the voice of your weeping and will give you strength to overcome your fears, anxiety, and frustration. There is no sin in crying out to God and pleading with Him over your distress. You may know some strong Christians who have suffered far worse and still consistently praise God throughout their trials. Learn from their example. Praise and honor are due to God through all circumstances. According to Spurgeon, "God's people may groan, but they may not grumble."[18]

Another place we find reference to Jesus crying, though it is uncertain if tears were actually shed, is on the cross when He cried, "My God, my God, why have You forsaken Me?" (Matthew 27:46). The Son, bearing all our sin and guilt, cried out to His Father in anguish because He was now separated from His Father. No matter what trial you face, or what hardship seems to be pressing upon you, the pain and suffering of the Father turning away from His innocent Son will never compare, let alone the punishment Christ endured. Your anguish will never be what Christ experienced, but you can cry out to the Father like He did. God will hear your pleas. Consider the words of David, "The Lord has heard my plea; the Lord accepts my prayer" (Psalm 6:9).

When times of weariness lay heavy upon you, turn to the Psalms for encouragement. There are Psalms of thanksgiving and praise, but there are also Psalms of sadness and sorrow. David had a gift of songwriting that expresses many of the emotions you may be feeling during your cancer journey. David faced circumstances of personal suffering, weariness from battle, pain, sorrow, joy, and thanksgiving. The following are some Psalms that offer comfort and assurance during what may seem like your darkest hour. I encourage you to read these when you are receiving treatment, fearful of the future, or when you are too tired to do anything but rest in bed. Memorize some of the key passages. Read the additional Psalms listed, if one particular emotion is pressing on you. Ask the Lord to fill you with peace as you meditate on the tender words of David and other Psalmists. Cry out to God because He is listening.

## CRIES OF JOY

Hopefully, there will be some very good days during your cancer journey. Good news can come in many forms—cancer disappearance in your scans, tolerating your treatment well, meeting a new friend in the infusion room, bonding with a spouse in a whole new way, or finding growth within your church body. Regardless of the news— good or bad—regardless of the circumstances, joy is abundant during this trial once you have the proper perspective. More importantly, being joyful is a command. "Rejoice in the Lord always; again I will say, Rejoice" (Philippians 4:4). Joy is the result of a relationship with your Heavenly Father, and nothing can steal that joy—not even cancer. If you are having difficulty finding joy, then open the Book of Psalms to get help. "Shout for joy to God, all the earth; sing the glory of His name; give to Him glorious praise!" (Psalm 66:1-2).

There are two reasons the Psalmist is shouting for joy. First, the Psalmist is joyful because God has not rejected his prayer. Second, he is joyful because God has not stopped loving him (Psalm 66:20). Notice that the Psalmist sings joyfully to God despite his difficulties. In verses 10-12, the Psalmist gives an account of these hardships,

## PSALM 66

*Shout for joy to God, all the earth; ² sing the glory of His name; give to Him glorious praise! ³ Say to God, "How awesome are Your deeds! So great is Your power that Your enemies come cringing to You. ⁴ All the earth worships You and sings praises to You; they sing praises to Your name." Selah*

*⁵ Come and see what God has done: He is awesome in His deeds toward the children of man...*

*⁸ Bless our God, O peoples; let the sound of His praise be heard, ⁹ who has kept our soul among the living and has not let our feet slip. ¹⁰ For You, O God, have tested us; You have tried us as silver is tried. ¹¹ You brought us into the net; You laid a crushing burden on our backs; ¹² You let men ride over our heads; we went through fire and through water; yet You have brought us out to a place of abundance...*

*¹⁶ Come and hear, all you who fear God, and I will tell what He has done for my soul. ¹⁷ I cried to Him with my mouth, and high praise was on my tongue. ¹⁸ If I had cherished iniquity in my heart, the Lord would not have listened. ¹⁹ But truly God has listened;*

*He has attended to the voice of my prayer. ²⁰ Blessed be God, because He has not rejected my prayer or removed His steadfast love from me!*

including a "crushing burden" and traversing through "fire" and "water" (Psalm 66:11-12). Yet, despite the pain, despite the sorrow, despite the hurt, the Psalmist is joyful because the Lord brought him "out to a place of abundance" (Psalm 66:12).

We can join the Psalmist in praising the Lord because He has also bestowed these two blessings on us—the Lord hears our prayer, and He loves His children. We have more confirmation in the New Testament that the Lord hears our prayer. "And this is the confidence that we have toward Him, that if we ask anything according to His will He hears us." (1 John 5:14). Not only does He hear our prayer and love us, but our Lord will not leave us in the despair and hardship of a trial. He will bring us to a place of abundance. Abundance could be in the form of a deeper understanding and more intimate relationship with Him, or it could be a more literal place of abundance by transporting us to Heaven.

Joy is our response to God's mercy and kindness, but the Psalmist also demonstrates two actions to follow joy. First, we should tell others what the Lord has done by sharing our joyful news and by daily expressing the joy in our hearts, giving God all the glory. "Come and hear, all you who fear God, and I will tell what He has done for my soul" (Psalm 66:16). This Psalmist remembered how the Lord cared for the people of Israel. He recalled the many tests and trials of the Israelites, but he concluded that the joy found in the Lord far exceeds the grief found through trial. Second, we must worship God. We must come before God and acknowledge His awesome deeds, our helpless state, and our love and adoration of Him. Worship is an act of submitting our entire hearts completely to God and giving Him all our praise.

The same God that was present with the Israelites and with the Psalmist is our God. He has not changed. His previous marvelous acts are still marvelous today. We can rejoice in what He *has* done and in what He *will* do. Much like the Psalmist, you will have a testimony to give during this journey, and you should share it with all who will listen. Your audience may be an individual believer, or it may be an entire church body who will receive encouragement from your words. Joy comes from the Lord despite trials, tests, hardships, or crushing burdens. As believers, we must recognize this joy and then act appropriately. As Paul wrote, "May the God of hope fill you with all joy and peace in believing, so that by the power of the Holy Spirit you may abound in hope" (Romans 15:13). Trials will come and go, but joy from the Lord will be with us always, and through that joy, we can find hope. For further reading, see Psalms 33, 47, and 145.

CRIES OF THANKSGIVING

Consider the statement, "Thank You, God, for the work You are doing through my trial of cancer." Is this declaration difficult for you? In Psalm 138, David gives thanks to God for His steadfast love and faithfulness (Psalm 138:2). David is thankful because he knows the Lord has been with him through times of trouble (Psalm 138:7). David sees the Lord's preservation in all his circumstances. He also acknowledges the Lord's purpose through all his trials. Consider that God is sovereign and has a plan for you through your cancer journey. Then consider how cancer is changing your relationship with God, forcing you to grow closer to Him and depend upon Him more.

When you call upon Him, the Lord will answer you and will strengthen you as He strengthened David (Psalm 138:3). In Psalm

105:4, the thankful heart is commanded to "Seek the Lord and His strength; seek His presence continually!" The Lord may not remove the burden, but strength from the Lord is an equally wonderful answer to prayer. His presence is of the most value. "'When you pass through the waters, I will be with you; and through the rivers, they shall not overwhelm you; when you walk through fire you shall not be burned, and the flame shall not consume you. For I am the Lord your

> ## PSALM 138
>
> *I give You thanks, O Lord, with my whole heart; before the gods I sing Your praise; ² I bow down toward Your holy temple and give thanks to Your name for Your steadfast love and Your faithfulness, for You have exalted above all things Your name and Your word. ³ On the day I called, You answered me; my strength of soul You increased. ⁴ All the kings of the earth shall give You thanks, O Lord, for they have heard the words of Your mouth, ⁵ and they shall sing of the ways of the Lord, for great is the glory of the Lord. ⁶ For though the Lord is high, He regards the lowly, but the haughty He knows from afar. ⁷ Though I walk in the midst of trouble, You preserve my life; You stretch out Your hand against the wrath of my enemies, and Your right hand delivers me. ⁸ The Lord will fulfill His purpose for me; Your steadfast love, O Lord, endures forever. Do not forsake the work of Your hands.*

God, the Holy One of Israel, your Savior'" (Isaiah 43:1-3). Notice, in this verse, the Lord acknowledges that trials *will* occur, and *when* they do, He will be with you. Strength through your cancer journey and comfort from a Savior walking beside you deserves an attitude of thanksgiving.

Therefore, give thanks with your "whole heart" (Psalm 138:1). The Lord requires all of you—not a small, convenient portion. When you give thanks with your whole heart, you are announcing to God, to yourself, and to the world that you have put your faith in the living God, and you trust Him to carry out His perfect plan for your life. You trust Him to strengthen you, preserve you, to stretch out His hand against your enemies, and deliver you (Psalm 138:7). Most importantly, you acknowledge that "the Lord will fulfill His purpose for me; your steadfast love, O Lord, endures forever" (Psalm 138:8). For further reading, see Psalms 105, 107, 118, and 136.

## CRIES OF FEAR

Fear is a powerful and crippling emotion. It is a plague of anxiety and insecurity with regard to some perceived danger. An example of fear in the Bible occurred when the disciples saw Jesus walking on water (Matthew 14:22-33). They were terrified because they thought Jesus was a ghost, but once the disciples heard and recognized His voice, they were immediately relieved. Peter demonstrated a bold act of faith by responding to Christ's call to come to Him, thus overcoming his fear and walking out to meet Christ on the water.

Cancer causes fear in us similar to the disciples' fear because it renders an individual with feelings of helplessness and the inability to be in control. You do not know exactly what to expect, and you do not know how you will feel. Treatments like radiation and chemotherapy can be very scary. King David said, "The Lord is my light and my salvation; whom shall I fear? The Lord is the stronghold of my life; of whom shall I be afraid?" (Psalm 27:1). Notice how David declares this with full confidence and even states this confidence in verse three, "Though an army encamp against me, my heart shall not fear; though war arise against me, yet I will be confident." David is confident because he has been rescued by the Lord in previous instances of danger (1 Samuel 17:37). Are you confident in the Lord? You can place your full trust in the Lord because He is your salvation and your saving grace. He has rescued you from the perils of spiritual death.

## PSALM 27

*The Lord is my light and my salvation; whom shall I fear? The Lord is the stronghold of my life; of whom shall I be afraid? [2]When evildoers assail me to eat up my flesh, my adversaries and foes, it is they who stumble and fall. [3]Though an army encamp against me, my heart shall not fear; though war arise against me, yet I will be confident. [4]One thing have I asked of the Lord, that will I seek after: that I may dwell in the house of the Lord all the days of my life, to gaze upon the beauty of the Lord and to inquire in His temple. [5]For He will hide me in His shelter in the day of trouble; He will conceal me under the cover of His tent; He will lift me high upon a rock. [6]And now my head shall be lifted up above my enemies all around me, and I will offer in His tent sacrifices with shouts of joy; I will sing and make melody to the Lord. [7]Hear, O Lord, when I cry aloud; be gracious to me and answer me! [8]You have said, "Seek my face." My heart says to You, "Your face, Lord, do I seek." [9]Hide not Your face from me. Turn not Your servant away in anger, O You who have been my help. Cast me not off; forsake me not, O God of my salvation! [10]For my father and my mother have forsaken me, but the Lord will take me in. [11]Teach me Your way, O Lord, and lead me on a level path because of my enemies. [12]Give me not up to the will of my adversaries; for false witnesses have risen against me, and they breathe out violence. [13]I believe that I shall look upon the goodness of the Lord in the land of the living! [14]Wait for the Lord; be strong, and let your heart take courage; wait for the Lord!*

If you are struggling with fear, then follow David's example throughout this Psalm. First, David seeks to be near the Lord and dwell in His house. "One thing have I asked of the Lord, that will I seek after: that I may dwell in the house of the Lord all the days of my life, to gaze upon the beauty of the Lord and to inquire in His temple" (Psalm 27:4). The absolute best place to find comfort is in the arms of Christ. Surround yourself with the Word and with fellow believers who can provide encouragement for you. Second, David asks the Lord to teach him. "Teach me your way, O Lord, and lead me on a level path because of my enemies" (Psalm 27:11). Learn everything you can about the Lord and the Scriptures, for the more you know about Him, the more you will trust Him.

Finally, David sings praises to the Lord. "And now my head shall be lifted up above my enemies all around me, and I will offer in His tent sacrifices with shouts of joy; I will sing and make melody to the Lord" (Psalm 27:6). Communion with God, learning His perfect ways, and rejoicing in Him will lead you to trust in the full authority of God and allow Him to be your stronghold during those fearful times.

Fear should only be a fleeting thought, and it should bring you to seek and trust Christ. We all have moments of anxiety, but they should be brief. If we truly look to Christ for all our hope, like Peter looked to Christ on the water and David found his confidence in the

Lord, then we will not be trapped or paralyzed by fear. Look at David's final actions in verse 14. "Wait for the Lord, be strong, and let your heart take courage; wait for the Lord!" Surround yourself with the Word of the Lord, be confident in the miracle He has already accomplished in your life, and sing your praises to God all with a heart of anticipation in what He will accomplish through the cancer journey. Memorize this verse and think of it when you are fearful. For further reading, see Psalms 18, 30, and 46.

## CRIES OF BOASTFULNESS

This type of crying may seem strange to you during the cancer journey, but cries of boastfulness are simply proclaiming what God is doing and what He will do. This can include very simple things, such as boasting in the beauty of His creation while walking outside. It could be adoration for God through a child's smile or laughter. Your boasting could be in the Lord's protection over you during your cancer treatments or in the fact that your pain is not severe. Overcoming fear can lead to a boastful heart, as well. "I sought the Lord, and He answered me and delivered me from all my fears" (Psalm 34:4).

We will never run out of praises for the Lord. They can be applied in every circumstance of our lives. As David said, "I will bless the Lord at all times; His praise shall continually be in my mouth"

## Psalm 34

*I will bless the Lord at all times; His praise shall continually be in my mouth. ² My soul makes its boast in the Lord; let the humble hear and be glad. ³ Oh, magnify the Lord with me, and let us exalt His name together! ⁴ I sought the Lord, and He answered me and delivered me from all my fears. ⁵ Those who look to Him are radiant, and their faces shall never be ashamed...¹⁰ The young lions suffer want and hunger; but those who seek the Lord lack no good thing. ¹¹ Come, O children, listen to me; I will teach you the fear of the Lord. ¹² What man is there who desires life and loves many days, that he may see good? ¹³ Keep your tongue from evil and your lips from speaking deceit. ¹⁴ Turn away from evil and do good; seek peace and pursue it. ¹⁵ The eyes of the Lord are toward the righteous and His ears toward their cry. ¹⁶ The face of the Lord is against those who do evil, to cut off the memory of them from the earth. ¹⁷ When the righteous cry for help, the Lord hears and delivers them out of all their troubles. ¹⁸ The Lord is near to the brokenhearted and saves the crushed in spirit. ¹⁹ Many are the afflictions of the righteous, but the Lord delivers him out of them all. ²⁰ He keeps all his bones; not one of them is broken. ²¹ Affliction will slay the wicked, and those who hate the righteous will be condemned. ²² The Lord redeems the life of His servants; none of those who take refuge in Him will be condemned.*

(Psalm 34:1). Praise is due to God in any dark time in your life, including your fight with cancer. If you are having a hard time finding things to boast about, then allow Jeremiah 9:23-24 to give you direction. "Thus says the Lord: 'Let not the wise man boast in his wisdom, let not the mighty man boast in his might, let not the rich man boast in his riches, but let him who boasts boast in this, that he understands and knows Me, that I am the Lord who practices steadfast love, justice, and righteousness in the earth.'"

Look back at the cross and remind yourself of what God has done for you through His Son. The Gospel message deserves an attitude of praise. Once you remember the Gospel, you will find many other things to boast about. Psalm 34 gives us just a few examples of things we can boast about: the Lord hears the cry of the righteous, He is near those who are brokenhearted, and He redeems the life of His servants (verses 15, 18, and 22). "Oh, taste and see that the Lord is good! Blessed is the man who takes refuge in Him!" (Psalm 34:8).

A boastful heart is also helpful to those around you, especially non-believers. "Those who look to Him are radiant, and their faces shall never be ashamed" (Psalm 34:5). Moses exhibited radiance after he was in the presence of the Lord (Exodus 34:29-35). Then, when leaving his communion with God, Moses would cover his face with a veil because he did not want the Israelites to see the light fading (2 Corinthians 3:13). Though this was a supernatural phenomenon with Moses, being away from God fades our "light," as well. When you look toward the Lord and seek Him, you will exhibit His light, and you will also "lack no good thing" (Psalm 34:10). Boasting is infectious and will soon be caught by those around you. "Oh, magnify the Lord with me, and let us exalt His name together!" (Psalm 34:3). For further reading, see Psalms 19, 29, 103, and 104.

CRIES OF HOPELESSNESS

"When I remember God, I moan; when I meditate, my spirit faints" (Psalm 77:3). The cancer journey may seem long and

## PSALM 77

*I cry aloud to God, aloud to God, and He will hear me. ² In the day of my trouble I seek the Lord; in the night my hand is stretched out without wearying; my soul refuses to be comforted. ³ When I remember God, I moan; when I meditate, my spirit faints. Selah*

*⁴ You hold my eyelids open; I am so troubled that I cannot speak. ⁵ I consider the days of old, the years long ago. ⁶ I said, "Let me remember my song in the night; let me meditate in my heart." Then my spirit made a diligent search: ⁷ "Will the Lord spurn forever, and never again be favorable? ⁸ Has His steadfast love forever ceased? Are His promises at an end for all time? ⁹ Has God forgotten to be gracious? Has He in anger shut up His compassion?" Selah*

*¹⁰ Then I said, "I will appeal to this, to the years of the right hand of the Most High." ¹¹ I will remember the deeds of the Lord; yes, I will remember Your wonders of old. ¹² I will ponder all Your work, and meditate on Your mighty deeds. ¹³ Your way, O God, is holy. What god is great like our God? ¹⁴ You are the God who works wonders; You have made known Your might among the peoples. ¹⁵ You with Your arm redeemed Your people, the children of Jacob and Joseph. Selah*

*¹⁶ When the waters saw You, O God, when the waters saw You, they were afraid; indeed, the deep trembled…¹⁹ Your way was through the sea, Your path through the great waters; yet Your footprints were unseen. ²⁰ You led Your people like a flock by the hand of Moses and Aaron.*

hopeless. Whether your treatment will last for six months or will be an indefinite cycle, you may wonder if God has "forgotten to be gracious" (Psalm 77:9). Perhaps you are asking the same questions the Psalmist asks in verses seven through nine. "Has His steadfast love forever ceased? Are His promises at an end for all time?" (Psalm 77:8). Entering a lengthy trial of suffering can be difficult. It is hard to understand why we must endure hardship and suffering, and we can sometimes wonder where God may be in all this.

Despite his grief, the Psalmist does not dwell in his present sorrow and suffering. Instead, he remembers all the Lord's past deeds and works. He doesn't allow his present circumstance to consume him, but instead he looks to the gracious and merciful works of the Lord. The Psalmist remembers what the Lord did for His chosen people by delivering them from the Egyptians. In Exodus 3:7, the Lord said, "'I have surely seen the affliction of my people who are in Egypt and have heard their cry because of their taskmasters.'" In your darkest hour, remember what the Lord has done for you. Despite your feelings of solitude and loneliness, God has never left you. He is the same today, yesterday, and tomorrow (Hebrews 13:8). You can "cry aloud to God" (Psalm 77:1) and know with full confidence that He will hear you, as He has heard the cries of all His children throughout eternity.

Recall Psalm 66, where the Psalmist remembered the past works of the Lord and cried out in joy. In Psalm 77, the Psalmist remembers the past works of the Lord as a way to combat hopelessness. Look back to your past to remember what the Lord has done for you. Your salvation is a miraculous work, and that alone should scatter all hopelessness and compel you to joy. Almighty God loved you enough to save you from your sins and from eternal death. "For while we were still weak, at the right time Christ died for the ungodly. For one will scarcely die for a righteous person—though perhaps for a good person one would dare even to die— but God shows His love for us in that while we were still sinners, Christ died for us" (Romans 5:6-8). For further reading, see Psalms 39, 56, 102, and 120.

My prayer for you during, and after, your treatment is that you will be able to praise the Lord as the psalmist did in Psalm 71:22-23:

> *I will also praise You with the harp*
> *for Your faithfulness, O my God;*
> *I will sing praises to You with the lyre,*
> *O Holy One of Israel.*
> *My lips will shout for joy,*
> *when I sing praises to You;*
> *my soul also, which You have redeemed.*

# CHAPTER FIVE

# FINDING JOY IN TRIALS

Tom's wife called our triage nurse early Monday morning. Over the weekend, Tom had developed a fever of 101 degrees Fahrenheit and had shaking chills. As a result, he had been in bed most of the weekend and had not eaten much food. He was weak and got dizzy with any type of activity. He was also coughing and experiencing some shortness of breath. The nurse asked Tom to come to our office right away for evaluation. His last chemotherapy for his stage IV lung cancer had been one week prior to this event, so his blood counts were at their lowest point. Upon his arrival, Tom appeared quite ill. The history of events, along with an assessment of him, suggested pneumonia. He needed to be admitted to the hospital so he could be closely monitored and receive IV antibiotics. Although he was not excited about a hospital stay, Tom was relieved to have help.

## UNEXPECTED EVENTS

During treatment, there may come a time when you need additional attention for an illness or complication. Receiving chemotherapy or radiation will make you more prone to infection, dehydration, and other problems. Cancer can also cause serious problems, such as blood clots or other emergencies which may require hospitalization. Additional health problems such as diabetes, heart conditions, and lung problems can all contribute to an increase in illness during treatment. The healthier you are overall, the easier your treatment will be.

Most oncologists will give instructions for when to call the office, and most offices will have an on-call provider to take phone calls when the office is closed. Reasons for calling generally include any of the following: fever, chills, shortness of breath, vomiting or diarrhea that cannot be controlled, and pain that cannot be controlled. Call your oncologist anytime you have concerns or questions. They are there to help you and would rather you call than to wait until things get worse. However, it is important to understand that a phone call is not the same as seeing the provider in the office. In the evenings, and at night, the only way to get immediate attention is through your local emergency department.

## DELAYS IN CHEMOTHERAPY

While it is important to stay close to schedule, your physician will delay chemotherapy if the side effects of chemotherapy become too risky. One of the most common reasons to delay chemotherapy is a low blood count. Most physicians have a set of acceptable values for the red blood cells, white blood cells, and platelets, as we discussed in Chapter 4. If the blood count values are too low, you may be at risk for infection or bleeding. In this case, delaying the chemotherapy will allow the bone marrow to recover from the previous treatment and start producing the appropriate blood cells again.

Other side effects can also prompt a delay in chemotherapy. For example, if you are suffering from moderate to severe mucositis (mouth sores), then giving more chemotherapy will cause the sores to worsen and could eventually jeopardize your ability to eat and drink properly. Since there is no "cure" for mouth sores, the best remedy is to hold the chemotherapy and allow the sores to heal.

Finally, your physician may delay chemotherapy because of infection. The "common cold" in someone with a good immune system is usually not a major problem. However, chemotherapy suppresses the immune system and can allow a simple viral or bacterial infection to become more severe. Adequate time must be given for the body to heal by delaying chemotherapy to avoid further complications.

INFECTION

Fever and chills are signs of infection and are the body's natural immune response to infection, whether the source is bacterial, viral, or fungal. In cancer patients, especially those receiving chemotherapy, the immune system is low and cannot fight infection very well. Also, treatment can lower the number of white blood cells in the body, which are responsible for fighting infection. If a patient does not have enough white blood cells, he will not be able to fight infection. Infection can be life-threatening without the tools to fight, so it is important to contact the physician at the first sign of infection. By definition, a fever is a temperature greater than 100.5 degrees Fahrenheit, and chills are characterized by shaking or exaggerated shivering of the body. Pay attention to other symptoms anytime fever or chills develop. A cough that produces phlegm or sputum may be a sign of pneumonia. Uncontrollable diarrhea may be a sign of a gastrointestinal infection. Pain with urination, or urinating more often, may be a sign of a urinary tract infection.

Infections can also be due to anything foreign being placed into the body. If the nursing staff has difficulty accessing your veins for chemotherapy delivery, or if the type of chemotherapy you are receiving requires a special pump for home chemotherapy delivery, then you may be encouraged to have a special type of catheter placed for easier chemotherapy delivery. A PICC line (peripherally-inserted central catheter) or a central port-a-cath is a device placed by a surgeon or interventional radiologist that provides intravenous access for an extended period of time. These devices are very useful for the staff, and they provide a bit of additional comfort for the patient. However, anything placed in the body that is foreign will carry a risk of infection. If a fever develops, then the device may be considered the source of infection.

If your provider suspects an infection, then you will likely be started on antibiotics. Antibiotics will only work against bacterial

## BESIDES INFECTION, WHAT OTHER PROBLEMS CAN BE CAUSED BY CENTRAL CATHETERS?

Central catheters can make chemotherapy delivery easier for both you and the nursing staff. However, in addition to the risk of infection, central catheters can also cause blood clots. A blood clot is a mass of thick, coagulated blood that becomes lodged in a blood vessel, usually a vein. A patient with a blood clot may have swelling and pain in the arm or neck on the side where the catheter is located. In some cases, the blood clot can become infected and cause fever. An ultrasound can be used to determine if a blood clot is present, and if so, blood thinning medications will be necessary for three to six months or longer, depending on how long the catheter is present. In the event of a blood clot, if the catheter continues to work properly, then it usually does not require removal. However, if the catheter is not working properly, or if it becomes infected, then it may have to be removed.

In some circumstances, the catheter can become blocked with a fibrous material, which is part of the body's response to a foreign object. Fibrous material is not the same as having a blood clot. Often, the catheter will continue to work as fluids or medications are being pushed in, as this will push the fibrous material away from the catheter, but it will not work for pulling blood out because the suctioning technique will pull the material toward the catheter, thus occluding it. In this situation, the catheter can be evaluated by a particular imaging study where dye is injected into the catheter and x-rays are taken. If fibrous material is present over the catheter tip, then the catheter can be injected with a medication to destroy the fibrous material, thus allowing catheter use to resume.

infections and will not be effective against viruses, but it can sometimes be difficult to distinguish between the two. There are many different antibiotics available, but each antibiotic is tailored to treat a specific type of bacteria. Bacteria that cause pneumonia will likely require a different antibiotic from the bacteria causing a urinary tract infection. Tests can be performed to identify the exact bacteria causing the infection, and other tests can then identify which antibiotic will provide the best treatment. The test results can take several days to obtain. Sometimes providers start patients on more than one antibiotic so that they can cover more bacteria when they are unsure of the exact cause of the infection.

If your white blood cells are low, then your provider may want you to be treated in the hospital with intravenous antibiotics and close nursing coverage. When your white blood cells are low, a simple infection can turn into a very severe infection within a matter of hours. Medications can also be used to stimulate your bone marrow to make more white blood cells, which will help your body fight the infection.

DEHYDRATION

Anna had been nauseated for three days. She received chemotherapy every three weeks for her ovarian cancer. Her physician had given her medication to help with nausea and vomiting after her last treatment. It seemed to be helping a little, but she was still having trouble with food. Everything she looked at, or smelled, caused her to feel nauseous. She tried to drink water, but it tasted like metal. As the days passed, she grew weaker. She was dizzy when she stood up, and she started to feel faint. Her husband brought her to our office to be evaluated. She was given intravenous fluids and additional anti-nausea medication. After three hours of fluids, the color was returning to her face, and she was beginning to feel stronger. She didn't realize just how dehydrated she had gotten.

Another common problem with cancer patients—especially those patients receiving treatment—is dehydration. If you are unable to eat or drink properly, or if you have nausea, vomiting, or diarrhea, you may become dehydrated. Signs and symptoms of dehydration include dry mouth, loss of energy, weakness, and lightheadedness. Severe dehydration may result in low blood pressure and may lead to fainting or loss of consciousness. Mild dehydration can usually be resolved by drinking more fluids—especially fluids with electrolytes, like common sports drinks. However, drinking fluids may be difficult if you are vomiting excessively or having severe diarrhea, so you may benefit from intravenous fluids which can be given in an infusion center or at the hospital. A hospital admission may be necessary to resolve the underlying cause of dehydration.

## Emergencies

Chest pain, difficulty breathing, and confusion are considered emergencies and should be handled in the emergency room. Chest pain could be a sign of a heart attack or blood clot. Shortness of breath, or difficulty breathing, could be a sign of infection, blood clots, or fluid present on the lung. Confusion could be a sign of stroke or cancer progression to the brain. These are just a few examples of emergencies, and they are not manageable over the phone, so it is best to go straight to the emergency room. If you are unable to get to the ER, then you may need to call 911 to have the paramedics come to your home.

I will never forget the day Beth was admitted to the hospital. She was brought into our office by her son. He told me that she wasn't acting herself and seemed confused. I knew Beth very well from her many treatments for her stage IV breast cancer. She was a lovely, jovial person who had never met a stranger. She could carry on a conversation with anyone and make them feel at ease. On this particular day, however, Beth was a completely different person. She was angry and mad.

Combining the history from the son with this obvious personality change, Beth was admitted to the hospital and evaluated with a brain MRI. The MRI showed metastatic disease present in the brain. In other words, her breast cancer had progressed to her brain.

After receiving radiation, Beth became her old self again. Later, I asked Beth if she knew what had happened. She said she knew she wasn't acting correctly, but she couldn't stop herself. This was quite an unexpected event for Beth, and it was considered an oncologic emergency.

## HOSPITAL ADMISSIONS

You may already be familiar with what happens during a hospital visit if you were in the hospital when your cancer was diagnosed. The hospital is a place for 24-hour monitoring and treatment. Admission to the hospital is based on your diagnosis and the severity of your illness. Whether admission to the hospital is through the emergency room or directly from your doctor's office, all admissions require an attending physician. The attending physician is responsible for coordinating and overseeing your care while you are hospitalized. This may be your oncologist, or it may be a primary care physician, such as an internist, family physician, or hospitalist.

A hospitalist is a physician who limits his practice to hospital-based patients. Often, family practitioners or internists will utilize a hospitalist when a patient is admitted to the hospital, as they may not feel comfortable dealing with a "sicker" patient, or they may not have the amount of time required to attend to a hospitalized patient. The attending physician will ask other physicians from various specialties to see you, depending on your needs. For example, when Mr. Allen was admitted to the hospital for pneumonia, our oncologist asked a pulmonologist (a specialist in lungs) to come and evaluate him. The pulmonologist decided on any testing or treatment Mr. Allen might require that specifically pertained to the pneumonia.

While you are in the hospital, many tests will be performed, many labs will be drawn, and there will be many interruptions by the nursing staff to evaluate you. Be patient and give the hospital staff your cooperation. Physicians often visit in the morning before they begin their office work, so they need daily lab work done early. Nurses follow the orders of the physicians, which can include an evaluation every four to six hours, even at night.

## TIPS WHILE HOSPITALIZED

1. Have a complete list of all your medications, including the name, dosage, amount you take, and when you take it. Also, have a list of all physicians whom you have seen recently and who are involved in your care.
2. Do not take any medications or pills without first asking the hospital staff.
3. If possible, have a responsible person with you most of the time. It is easy to become confused while you are in the hospital, so a second pair of ears and eyes is always helpful.
4. It is okay to question the medical staff regarding your care, but do so with grace and gentleness. Errors do occur, but often due to understaffing, not incompetence or negligence.
5. Limit your visitors. You will be busy enough in the hospital and should get as much rest as you can. If you have a supportive family or church, let them know a good time to visit so you still have plenty of time to rest. Asking them to call instead of visit may be easier on you and them. Finally, anyone who is ill should not be visiting you.

Once you are discharged from the hospital, you will be sent home with a list of instructions. These instructions may include new medications you need to take, orders for special equipment, or appointments to follow-up with your physician. The nurse will explain all of the discharge instructions before you leave. However, there may be a lot of information, and it can be confusing, so ask questions if you do not understand something.

ENCOURAGEMENT FROM THE WORD

*Count it all joy, my brothers, when you meet trials of various kinds, for you know that the testing of your faith produces steadfastness. And let steadfastness have its full effect, that you may be perfect and complete, lacking in nothing.* (James 1:2-4)

David may have played the harp in his praise and worship to the Lord, but Margaret played the flute. The Lord blessed her with a gift of music, and she spent most of her life teaching music to others and using her gifts for the glory of the Lord. When she developed pancreatic cancer, the music did not stop. In fact, she found more reasons to sing and worship. The last few months of her life were spent preparing her students for a concert, worshipping with her brothers and sisters in Christ, and enjoying every moment with her children and grandchildren. She was filled with joy each day as she prepared to go home to her Savior.

Cancer and joy? The two words go together like oil and water. The world would say you are crazy if you use those two words together in the same sentence. The world would really laugh if you insert the word "cancer" into James's verse - "Consider it pure joy when you meet cancer..." Perhaps it seems strange, but when you look at cancer as a trial—yes, a particularly tough one—then maybe it will not seem so frightening.

No, this won't be your first instinct. The treatment can be challenging, the anxiety and fear associated with cancer can be paralyzing, and the strain on relationships can be difficult. Unexpected events like hospital admissions may anger you and leave you shaking your fists, wondering when the gunfire will stop. Trials are never easy, but the good thing about experiencing a trial is that it forces us to rely on our Heavenly Father. He is our comforter in times of weakness, our strength when we are powerless, and our guide when we feel lost or confused.

> Trials are never easy, but the good thing about experiencing a trial is that it forces us to rely on our Heavenly Father.

Look at the verse from James again and focus on the goal of the trial. The goal of any trial is not to make you suffer, but to draw you closer to God and allow Him to make you perfect and complete. Perfection in us is a constant, timely work that requires many trials. James uses the example of a farmer waiting patiently for his fruit to be produced (James 5:7-8). For any fruit to grow, it must have sunshine, rain, and time. There will be many sunny days in our lives when we see the blessings of our Lord and rejoice, but without the rain, we will never produce fruit. Solomon also recognized varying seasons in our life. "For everything there is a season, and a time for every matter under heaven…a time to weep, and a time to laugh" (Ecclesiastes 3:1, 4).

Those times of weeping are important in the ultimate goal of our Lord—to perfect us. R.C. Sproul in his book, *Surprised by Suffering,* describes the Christian life as a pilgrimage moving "from faith to faith, from strength to strength, and from grace to grace. It moves toward a crescendo. Ironically, the progress passes through suffering and tribulation."[19] No, the Lord does not promise an easy walk, but He does promise to keep pruning the branches so that the good fruit will be produced. It is our job to trust Him.

Perhaps the greatest example of human suffering in the Bible, second only to Christ's death on the cross, is found in the Book of Job. James 5:11 says, "Behold, we consider those blessed who remained steadfast. You have heard of the steadfastness of Job, and you have seen the purpose of the Lord, how the Lord is compassionate and merciful." Job was a righteous man who was also very wealthy. He had ten children, many servants, and numerous livestock. Beyond all of these things, the best asset Job had was that he found favor with God. Because of this, God drew Satan's attention to Job as an example of an upright man. In an effort to prove Job's integrity as false, Satan challenged God to see if Job was really a righteous man. In one tragic day, Job lost his vast wealth of livestock, and all of his children were killed in a whirlwind. Instead of sinning, during this intense time of trial, Job 1:20 says he "...fell on the ground and worshiped" the Lord.

In all circumstances, especially in trials, we must worship the Lord as Job did. We must accept the unforeseen, unplanned, and unwelcomed events as part of God's plan for us. What work is He trying to accomplish in us? How can we use this trial to shift our focus to Christ

> We must accept the unforeseen, unplanned, and unwelcomed events as part of God's plan for us.

and grow closer to Him? Our Heavenly Father is a loving God who desires to "perfect" us, as the verse in James states (James 1:2-4). Worshipping God is a sign of obedience and a sign of thankfulness for all of the undeserved blessings He has given us. Worshipping God is also a sign of trust. As Sproul explains, "Job's trust wavered, but it never died. He mourned. He cried. He protested. He questioned. He even cursed the day of his birth. But he clutched tightly to his only possible hope, his trust in God."[19]

Not only did Job worship the Lord, but he also acknowledged that everything he had belonged to God. In Job 1:21, he says, "... The Lord gave, and the Lord has taken away; blessed be the name of the Lord." We must follow Job's example by recognizing that our health, our family, and our possessions are gifts from the Lord. We are simply caretakers of the gifts and blessings He chooses to bestow on us. God provided you this life and gave you the talents and skills that earned you the job, which gave you the financial resources to purchase your possessions. The same applies to your body and health. "Or do you not know that your body is a temple of the Holy Spirit within you, whom you have from God? You are not your own, for you were bought with a price. So glorify God in your body" (1 Corinthians 6:19-20).

Understanding that you own, or possess, nothing can help you during times of trial. When we acknowledge that we own nothing, then its disappearance will not be shocking. Consider the instruction from Christ in Matthew 6:19-21, "Do not lay up for yourselves treasures on earth, where moth and rust destroy and where thieves break in and steal, but lay up for yourselves treasures in heaven, where neither moth nor rust destroys and where thieves do not break in and steal. For where your treasure is, there your heart will be also."

Our treasure does not lie in large amounts of land, possessions, children, or even a healthy life; rather, our treasure lies with God and can be found in spending our life to glorify Him.

Let us again revisit the story of Job, for his trial did not end with the loss of his fortune or the death of his children. Satan challenged the Lord again, only this time to strike at Job personally. Job developed a very painful and visible disease. Though we have no indication of the type of disease, it could be as though Job developed cancer. Even in this, Job did not sin. Twice we are told that Job did not sin, even though his trial was great. His friends, and even his wife, assumed that Job had sinned greatly for the tragic events that occurred, but Job maintained his innocence. To try and understand why all this was occurring, Job requested an audience with God to plead his case. God granted his request but began with a series of questions that humbled Job and should humble us. "Where were you when I [God] laid the foundation of the earth? Tell me, if you have understanding. Who determined its measurements—surely you know!" (Job 38:4-5). This monologue captures God's omniscient and omnipotent attributes, and we cannot possibly fathom His all-knowing wisdom. Job was awed by God's power and majesty. He sought forgiveness for questioning God and not understanding God's ways. In response, God blessed Job with twice as much as he had previously and granted him a full life.

Notice in Job 1:8 and Job 2:3 that it is the Lord who brings Satan's attention to Job. This is just another example of our God exercising His control. Nothing can happen to us without His permission. Does it seem harsh that God would draw Satan's attention to His chosen people? Though we may not understand

> Nothing can happen to us without His permission.

the purpose of the trial, as Job did not understand why he was made to suffer, we can trust God to bring us closer to Him *through* the trial. "Indeed, we felt that we had received the sentence of death. But that was to make us rely not on ourselves but on God who raises the dead" (2 Corinthians 1:9). Our God expects full reliance on Him. He desires a deeper relationship and a stronger faith in Him.

At the end of Job's trial, he was given twice as much as before, and he was also blessed in his latter days (Job 42). More important than Job's health and fortune being restored, Job was blessed with a better understanding of who God really is. He recognized that God is good and just, and he was better able to see that God is all he needed to be satisfied in any circumstance. Notice Job's response after the Lord humbles him. "I know that You can do all things, and that no purpose of Yours can be thwarted. 'Who is this that hides counsel without knowledge?' Therefore I have uttered what I did not understand, things too wonderful for me, which I did not know" (Job 42:2-3).

Job asked God why he suffered, yet in the entire monologue from God, no answer was given to Job. God does not need to answer our questions, though I don't think He minds us asking, as long as it is with a humble heart. Perhaps a more important question to ask God is not "why," but rather "what." What is the purpose of this trial, and how can He complete you and perfect you through it? Perhaps we can comfort another patient, or maybe the salvation of a family member can be achieved. You can only understand His ways if you ask Him to reveal them to you and ask Him to give you the wisdom to understand. How often do we utter things which we do not know? How often do we assume the worst, when God's way is really the best? His divine purpose for our life is something we cannot question.

Romans 5:3-5 reminds us to rejoice in our sufferings. "More than that, we rejoice in our sufferings, knowing that suffering produces endurance, and endurance produces character, and character produces hope, and hope does not put us to shame, because God's love has been poured into our hearts through the Holy Spirit who has been given to us." We rejoice because we have hope. Our hope is in Christ. Though our physical bodies may suffer, we can rejoice in the new creation God has formed in us and in the fact that our lives belong to Him. Though cancer can be a very difficult trial, our end result will be praise, honor, and glory given to Christ if we keep the faith. God can do more than we can ever think or imagine. "Now to Him who is able to do far more abundantly than all that we ask or think, according to the power at work within us, to Him be glory in the church and in Christ Jesus throughout all generations, forever and ever. Amen" (Ephesians 3:20-21).

# CHAPTER SIX

# FINDING GRACE IN DAILY LIFE

The six cycles of chemotherapy had finally come to an end. Michael was happy to be finished with his treatment and was ready to get back to his usual way of life. He missed playing ball with the guys at the gym, and he didn't like having to be careful of illness around his grandchildren. When Michael saw his physician, he wanted to know what the next step would be. The physician explained that he would now enter a phase of surveillance, which was a period of close observation to make sure the cancer did not recur or to catch the cancer early if it did recur. Surveillance included periodic physical exams, blood work, and radiographic imaging. Michael was a little nervous. He didn't want the lymphoma to have an opportunity to grow. Would the surveillance of the cancer be harder than the treatment itself?

## CANCER SURVEILLANCE

Once all cancer treatment is complete—including chemotherapy, surgery, or radiation—your cancer will be monitored by the oncologist for a period of time. The longer you are in remission, or "cancer free," the more likely it is that your cancer will never return. For the first two years, cancer surveillance will occur more often and will include more testing, generally, every three months. After the first two years, the interval between exams and tests will be lengthened. After about five years, surveillance will drop to once per year and could potentially even cease.

There are some general guidelines that physicians follow during the surveillance period that are established by the National Comprehensive Cancer Network (NCCN)[20], but most physicians have also tailored cancer surveillance based on their own experiences. Surveillance is based on the type of cancer and the stage of the cancer. For example, surveillance of an early-stage breast cancer usually only requires mammography every six months. Alternatively, a more advanced lung cancer may require CT scans every three to six months. Some cancer types will also have specific labs, called tumor markers, which may aid the physician in surveillance.

## CLINICAL EXAM

The history and physical exams are the most important parts of surveillance. There are specific signs and symptoms the physician will be looking for, based on the cancer type. Communicating to the physician any problems or concerns you have may provide important information to help diagnose cancer recurrence early. There are also findings on physical exams which can aid the physician in diagnosis. These findings can then lead the physician to order imaging studies or lab tests. For example, enlarged lymph nodes in a patient with lymphoma is a concern and will likely lead to testing that can help confirm, or rule out, the recurrence of lymphoma. Randomly ordering scans or lab tests can sometimes lead to discovering abnormal, but not necessarily malignant or dangerous, findings that then require more imaging and testing.

Imaging

Cancer imaging is a broad, advancing technology. In conventional imaging, energy in the form of x-rays, ultrasound, or magnetic fields are sent into the patient from the outside, and the resultant "shadows" are recorded and displayed on a screen. Newer imaging techniques using nuclear energy allow the patient to "emit" information based on the injecting, ingesting, or inhaling of a particular radioactive material. Both techniques provide specific, yet different, information, and the techniques for performing these imaging studies will vary.

Imaging studies must always be matched with the history and physical exam of the patient. Before ordering any imaging study, the physician or practitioner should have a question they are trying to answer, since different imaging modalities will give different types of information. For example, in a patient complaining of leg pain, the physician must decide if he is looking for a problem with the bone, such as a fracture. Imaging for the bones is best done by plain x-ray. However, if the physician is concerned about a blood clot causing the leg pain, then an x-ray would not be helpful. Instead, an ultrasound is the imaging study of choice when looking for a blood clot in the leg. Inappropriate imaging studies can lead to a delay in diagnosis, or even a misdiagnosis. It is also very expensive to order tests that will not be helpful.

Because there are many different types of imaging techniques, the preparation, specific setup, and results for each can vary. The imaging facility should provide you with directions for each test, including whether you can eat or drink prior to testing, what time to arrive, how to dress, and if there is contrast dye to be taken. Some imaging studies require intravenous contrast dye, which will require evaluation of kidney function prior to the test being performed. Other imaging studies require drinking of the contrast dye at a specific time before the picture is taken.

The following are the most common imaging studies used in cancer treatment. These same tests can be used in other diagnoses or diseases (for example, an ultrasound is used in pregnancy), so the information given will pertain more to cancer and how the physician may use various imaging techniques throughout cancer treatment and surveillance.

## PLAIN X-RAY (TRADITIONAL X-RAY)

Radiation type: X-ray

How it works: X-rays are very short wavelengths of electromagnetic radiation that are absorbed by structures in the body to produce an image. X-rays are absorbed at varying rates based on the electron density of the structure. Bones absorb the most, and therefore, appear white. Air does not absorb x-rays easily, and therefore, appears black. Other areas, such as muscle and blood, usually appear in varying degrees of gray.

Use in cancer: Plain x-ray imaging has many functions for the cancer patient. It can be used in the form of a chest x-ray for the evaluation, or surveillance, of the lungs by looking for nodules or lesions present. Plain x-ray imaging is commonly used for the evaluation of the bones by looking for cancerous lesions if the patient complains of bone pain. Finally, a very specific type of x-ray imaging is the mammogram, which is used for the screening and detection of breast cancer.

COMPUTED TOMOGRAPHY (CT) OR COMPUTERIZED AXIAL TOMOGRAPHY (CAT)

Radiation type: X-ray

How it works: CT scanning is similar to plain x-ray imaging, but CT scanning is more sensitive to small differences in x-ray absorption, resulting in better resolution. CT scanning requires many x-ray images from different angles that are then pieced together by a computer to create cross-sectional images, or "slices." The use of contrast dye (either oral or intravenous) allows structures, that are otherwise invisible, to be seen.

Use in cancer: CT scans are useful for the evaluation of the structures of the body and are more precise than plain x-ray imaging. CT imaging is most commonly used to evaluate cancer before, and during, treatment to see

## I AM ALLERGIC TO CONTRAST DYE. HOW WILL THAT AFFECT THE IMAGING STUDY MY DOCTOR HAS ORDERED?

Contrast dye is often used in CT scanning as a way to capture structures that are not well visualized. Patients who are allergic to shellfish may also have an allergy to contrast dye. A mild allergic reaction generally includes fever, chills, generalized itching, or rash. More severe allergies include shortness of breath, a drop in blood pressure, or a loss of consciousness. Medications can be given to patients with mild to moderate allergies, including antihistamines and steroids. These should prevent an allergic reaction from occurring. For patients with a severe allergy to contrast dye, it is best to avoid use of the dye. The CT scan can be performed without contrast, or another imaging technique should be used.

how an area is responding. After treatment is complete, CTs are used to make sure the cancer has not recurred. For even more data, the CT scan can be combined with PET imaging.

ULTRASOUND

Radiation type: None

How it works: Ultrasound relies on high frequency sound waves to travel through the body and produce "echoes," which are detected and converted into an electrical signal. Ultrasound waves pass easily through fluid, but not through solid structures like bones. When sound waves encounter two different structures that absorb the waves differently, the resultant image is created by the variance in the echoes.

Use in cancer: Ultrasounds are most commonly used to distinguish between fluid or solid structures. Some common examples include evaluating the liver where suspicious lesions can be identified as fluid-filled or solid, or evaluating a suspicious breast mass. Another common use of ultrasounds, though not specifically related to a type of cancer, is for the diagnosis of blood clots in the legs.

## MAGNETIC RESONANCE IMAGING (MRI)

Radiation type: None

How it works: MRI relies on a magnetic field and radio waves to produce detailed images of structures in the body. Additionally, contrast agents can be used to enhance these structures. The disadvantage to the MRI is that certain foreign objects in the body, like pacemakers and metal plates/clips, may not be compatible with MRI usage. In particular, metal objects that are magnetic are contraindicated with MRI use.

Use in cancer: MRIs are useful for the evaluation of the structures of the body and can give more detailed information over CT scanning. Virtually any part of the body can be evaluated by MRI, but in cancer imaging, it is more commonly used for the brain, spinal cord, liver, and bones. Breast MRI is a relatively new imaging technique and a fast growing standard in certain breast cancer diagnoses, especially those that are caused by the BRCA mutations (recall the explanation of hereditary breast cancer in Chapter 1).

## POSITRON EMISSION TOMOGRAPHY (PET)

Radiation type: Gamma ray

How it works: Radioactive imaging requires a naturally occurring radioactive isotope to be "tagged," or attached, to a specific substance in the body. In the most common PET imaging, a fluorine-18 radioactive isotope is attached to a glucose molecule and injected into the body. The glucose molecule is then taken into the cell as food since all tissues require food in the form of glucose. Food is particularly important to cancer cells, since they are replicating at a high rate and require more glucose than normal cells in the body. A scanner then detects what tissues have taken up the glucose molecule, and the images are displayed on a computer screen. After the imaging is complete, the radioactive isotope decays within a few hours, and it will be virtually gone 24 hours after the material was injected. Diabetics are at a disadvantage with PET scanning because the blood glucose level must be normal before the radioactive material can be injected.

Use in cancer: The PET scan is a valuable tool in the diagnosis, staging, and monitoring of cancer. PET imaging is often used at the beginning of a cancer diagnosis to see the various locations of cancer in the body so that staging can be determined. Then it is used periodically throughout treatment to see how the cancer is responding. For more accurate information, the PET scan can be combined with CT imaging.

BONE SCAN

Radiation type: Gamma ray

How it works: Similar to the PET scan, a bone scan requires a radioactive isotope to be attached to a bone scanning agent. The most commonly used isotope in this study is the technetium-99m. This agent will be taken up by the bone and will allow for specific imaging of the bone.

Use in cancer: The bone scan is best used for the evaluation of bone structures and the presence of cancer in the bones. It is most helpful in evaluating metastatic disease of the bone (the spread of cancer to the bones), but it can also be useful in diseases like multiple myeloma. The bone scan is often combined with plain x-rays for even better evaluation. As technology improves, the bone scan is being replaced by a PET scan using sodium fluoride F-18 as the isotope. The resultant image is more sensitive for bone lesions.

RADIATION EXPOSURE

Michelle was now in her second year of surveillance for stage III ovarian cancer. Her physician utilized CT scanning in conjunction with the clinical exam and tumor marker test. Michelle was hesitant to have the CT scan done because of the amount of radiation exposure associated with this form of imaging. Her physician explained to her how important the test was in her situation. She decided to do some research so that she could make an informed decision about having the CT scan performed.

The amount of radiation associated with x-rays, CT scans, or nuclear scans is a valid concern, and the risk of the scan must always be compared with the benefit. Radiation is simply defined as the emission of energy through particles or waves. It is measured in Sieverts, which is a unit of measurement that combines the amount of radiation absorbed and the medical effects of that type of radiation. We absorb small amounts of natural radiation each day in our normal activities, such as eating a banana (0.1 microsieverts), sleeping next to someone (0.05 microsieverts), or flying in an airplane (20-40 microsieverts). Simple x-rays also have a small amount of radiation exposure. A dental x-ray contains five microsieverts, and a chest x-ray contains twenty microsieverts. As the imaging study becomes more complex, the amount of absorbed radiation increases. A CT scan of the chest contains approximately 7000 microsieverts, and a PET/CT scan contains approximately 25,000 microsieverts. As we continue up the spectrum, one sievert (or one million microsieverts) in a short period of time (minutes to hours) can cause radiation sickness, and eight sieverts (eight million microsieverts) will cause death.[21, 22]

During cancer surveillance, CT scans and PET/CT scans are performed anywhere from every three to six months. What concerns most patients about imaging studies is the risk of developing cancer from repeated exposure to ionizing radiation. The lowest recorded dose of radiation linked to a risk of developing cancer is receiving 100,000 microsieverts of radiation in a time period of one year. The best advice when considering imaging studies is to weigh the risks and benefits. A PET/CT scan can give an amazing amount of information, which is important when receiving chemotherapy or radiation. However, sometimes a CT scan can be used instead of a combination PET/CT scan. This will decrease the amount of radiation exposure, but it will not give as much data. Also remember that ultrasound and MRI do not carry the same radiation hazard and are good alternatives when the image will give adequate information.

LABORATORY TESTING

As complex as the world of imaging may seem, laboratory testing is equally as complex and is constantly advancing. Oncologists use a variety of laboratory tests to monitor your cancer during treatment and in surveillance. Like any test, there can be some margin of error, which means the physician must use the history, physical examination, and sometimes imaging studies to properly interpret lab tests.

Laboratory testing is subject to many criteria for the results to be interpreted properly. To ensure the test will be run and interpreted properly, all persons involved in the process must have an understanding of the protocols for the particular test being performed. Some tests require preparation by the patient, such as fasting for twelve hours prior.

There are also specific directions the laboratory personnel must follow to ensure the proper collection and testing of the specimen. For example, all tests require proper collection containers for the test to be performed and evaluated correctly. Some tests require more specific action, such as multiple draws that must be done at specific time intervals. Finally, once the specimen is collected, it must be processed properly. Some samples must be frozen, while others are stored at room temperature. As you can see, there is more to laboratory testing than just the patient's presence and collection of the specimen.

In cancer patients, laboratory testing can be both basic and complex. We've already discussed the complete blood count (CBC) in detail as part of the clinician's monitoring of treatment and side effects (Chapter 4). The CBC can give some data in cancer surveillance, as well. It is very important in patients with leukemia or lymphoma, as it monitors the white blood cells (WBCs). For example, in chronic lymphocytic leukemia (CLL), the physician will monitor the WBCs to watch for an elevation or a trend upward. They will also monitor the particular WBC called the lymphocyte.

The CBC can be used in other cancer surveillance, like colon cancer. For example, if the hemoglobin begins to drop, thus rendering the patient anemic, then the physician may wonder if there is blood loss present in the intestinal tract. Blood loss in the intestinal tract could be a sign of cancer recurrence. With these two examples, it is important to remember that a particular disease may be present, and the lab may not show any abnormalities. Colon cancer may be present, and the CBC can be perfectly normal. Lymphoma may recur, and the CBC may show no evidence.

Another basic test utilized by the oncologist is the chemistry panel. This is actually a combination of several tests, but it generally includes evaluation of the electrolytes (sodium, potassium, chloride, magnesium, etc.), the kidney function, and the liver function. While often used during cancer treatment as a measurement of safety during chemotherapy delivery, the chemistry panel can also be used during surveillance. For example, if the liver function tests become elevated, then the physician may be prompted to order tests or imaging studies to evaluate the liver. There are many reasons for elevation in the liver function tests, such as excessive alcohol consumption, or medications like cholesterol-lowering drugs, so the test is simply a tool to aid the physician, not a way to diagnosis cancer recurrence.

There are more complex tests available for cancer surveillance and diagnosis. For our purposes, I will simply mention two types of testing—tumor markers and the bone marrow biopsy. Both of these tests are more advanced than the CBC and typical chemistry panel. They are usually reserved for the oncology setting, although some primary care offices are drawing tumor markers more often.

Advanced laboratory testing can also be performed on the actual cancer cells from the biopsy, but this is a highly specific topic and an area that still requires more research.

## TUMOR MARKERS

Judy called our office each day, eagerly awaiting the results from her tumor marker test. She had been diagnosed with stage III breast cancer a year previously, and she had finished all her treatments about six months later. She was anxious about the result, and she didn't realize that it took a couple of days for the lab to be processed. Finally, we had the result. I called

## MY TUMOR MARKER CAME BACK ELEVATED. DOES THAT MEAN MY CANCER HAS RECURRED?

Rather than looking at a specific number, your physician will monitor the tumor marker for a trend. For example, a falling tumor marker during treatment is a good sign of cancer response to that treatment. A rising tumor marker is often a sign that the treatment may not be working, or in the case of surveillance, that the cancer has recurred. Tumor markers are subject to many changes in the body and are not a specific sign of cancer. Often, tumor markers can be elevated for infection or inflammation. Because the tumor marker is sensitive to cancer, an elevated tumor marker will prompt your physician to order imaging studies to further evaluate the cancer.

her right away to let her know the good news. Her tumor marker was in the normal range. She was relieved.

Tumor markers are substances found in the body that are produced by cancer cells. They are best utilized once a cancer diagnosis is made as an indicator of treatment response, or during surveillance for the detection of cancer recurrence. Tumor markers can also be produced in response to some benign conditions, such as infection or inflammation, which means tumor markers are not a specific diagnosis of cancer. There are also examples of the tumor marker remaining in the normal range despite a cancer diagnosis or cancer recurrence. Therefore, the measurement of tumor markers should not replace the standard procedure for biopsy when diagnosing cancer. The following is a list of the most common tumor markers.[23, 24] This list is certainly not exhaustive, as many markers exist and more are being developed or improved.

PROSTATE SPECIFIC ANTIGEN (PSA)

Major cancer type: Prostate

Other information: The PSA is also used as a screening test in the primary care setting. Besides cancer, the PSA can be elevated when the prostate is enlarged or infected.

## CARCINOEMBRYONIC ANTIGEN (CEA)

Major cancer type: Colon

Other information: The CEA can be increased in inflammatory bowel disease, such as Crohn's or Ulcerative colitis, cirrhosis, pancreatitis, or lung disease.


## CA 27-29

Major cancer type: Breast

Other information: The CA 15-3 is another tumor marker for breast cancer. It measures the same marker as the CA 27-29, it just does so in a slightly different way.


## CA-125

Major cancer type: Ovarian, Endometrial

Other information: The CA-125 can also be elevated in pregnancy, pelvic inflammation, pancreatitis, inflammation of the peritoneal cavity or fluid present in the peritoneal cavity. The CA 72-4 is a newer tumor marker being studied for ovarian cancer and pancreatic cancer, but its efficacy is not yet known.

## CA 19-9

Major cancer type: Pancreatic

Other information: This marker may also be used for colon, gastric, liver, or biliary cancer. The CA 19-9 can also be elevated in conditions such as pancreatitis, gallstones, and cirrhosis.

## HUMAN CHORIONIC GONADOTROPIN (HCG)

Major cancer type: Testicular, Trophoblastic

Other information: Though not technically classified as a "tumor marker," this hormonal test is increased in testicular, ovarian, liver, and stomach cancers. In the primary care setting, the hCG is commonly evaluated to determine pregnancy.

## ALPHA-FETOPROTEIN (AFP)

Major cancer type: Liver

Other information: The AFP can be elevated in viral hepatitis, cirrhosis, and GI tumors. It is also useful in certain types of testicular cancers.

## BETA-2 MICROGLOBULIN (B2M)

Major cancer type: CLL, Multiple myeloma, Lymphoma

Other information: The Beta-2 microglobulin is also used to evaluate patients with kidney disease.

## BONE MARROW BIOPSY

The bone marrow biopsy and aspiration is a test of the bone marrow, which is the production site for the blood cells of the body (the red blood cells, white blood cells, and platelets). The bone marrow is located in the large bones of the pelvis or sternum, and the pelvis is the most common location for the test to be performed. The bone marrow gives information regarding the amount of cells being produced and whether the cells are maturing appropriately. Most often, the bone marrow biopsy is performed when abnormalities are detected in the blood cells on a CBC. While evaluation of the bone marrow is mostly for detecting blood disorders, it can also be used for the detection of certain infections. For the cancer patient, the bone marrow biopsy is part of the diagnosis and surveillance for leukemia, lymphoma, and multiple myeloma.

The procedure is a two-part process involving the collection of a fluid that looks like blood (called the aspiration) and a more solid material (called the biopsy). All together, the procedure can be done in the office under local anesthesia. Occasionally, the physician can give mild sedation, but general anesthesia is not necessary. The patient will be placed on their side or on their stomach for access to the large pelvic bone. After local anesthesia is given, a needle will be placed into the bone. Most often, the fluid portion is collected first, and then the biopsy. Once the procedure is complete, a pressure-type bandage is applied, and the patient is free to go home. Complications to watch for are bleeding and infection. In general, patients tolerate the procedure well and only have mild discomfort at the site after it is complete.

ENCOURAGEMENT FROM THE WORD

*So to keep me from becoming conceited because of the surpassing greatness of the revelations, a thorn was given me in the flesh, a messenger of Satan to harass me, to keep me from becoming conceited. Three times I pleaded with the Lord about this, that it should leave me. But He said to me, "My grace is sufficient for you, for My power is made perfect in weakness." Therefore I will boast all the more gladly of my weaknesses, so that the power of Christ may rest upon me. For the sake of Christ, then, I am content with weaknesses, insults, hardships, persecutions, and calamities. For when I am weak, then I am strong.* (2 Corinthians 12: 7-10)

Throughout the New Testament, we see Paul as a strong minister of the Gospel who spends his life on the road traveling and preaching. He faces many trials, including torture, hunger, shipwrecks, imprisonment, and persecution (2 Corinthians 11:23-25, 1 Corinthians 4:11-12). Despite all of these trials, Paul's teachings and letters make up the majority of the New Testament. He is the author of thirteen books of the New Testament and is considered one of the most prominent figures in Christianity.

In 2 Corinthians 12, we discover that Paul had a "thorn" in his flesh. There is some speculation as to the nature of this "thorn." It has been theorized that Paul suffered from a disease of the optic nerve (the nerve that controls eyesight), and that he was afflicted with this after his encounter with the bright light on the road to Damascus. In Galatians 4:13, Paul admits to having a "bodily ailment" that may have pertained to his eyesight (Galatians 4:15). Another theory says Paul suffered with an epileptic type of disease or seizure disorder.

Still another plausible theory is that the affliction was not an illness rather, it was an individual causing problems in Paul's ministry. John MacArthur, in his sermon, "The Sufficiency of God's Grace," interprets the "thorn" as an individual who was leading the opposition in the Corinthian church, thus leading the followers away from God's truth and the truth Paul had been teaching.[25] Regardless of the affliction, for it could have easily been a diagnosis like cancer, it is more important to understand that Paul asked for the "thorn" to be removed, Paul did not receive his request, and still Paul was satisfied with this answer because he knew Christ would sustain him through his life, ministry, and any trial he might face.

Paul not only asked for the thorn to be removed, but he pleaded. From this, we might infer that the affliction was debilitating and bothersome for Paul. There is no mention of him pleading for the Lord's intervention in all his other calamities, even when he was lashed, beaten, and stoned (2 Corinthians 11:24-25). Yet he was persistent and asked the Lord to remove this thorn three times. Paul did not question the Lord's abilities, and neither should we, especially His ability to heal, for there are many examples throughout the Old and New Testament of God's healing.

Jesus healed many people during His life and ministry, and His disciples were also given the ability to heal people. In Mark 2 we find a man who wanted to be healed of his paralysis. His caretakers were so persistent that they lowered him through the roof of the house just to get to Christ. Later, in Mark's account of Christ's ministry, we find another example of persistence in a woman who wanted to be healed so badly she made her way through the crowd to touch Christ's garments (Mark 5). As mentioned in Chapter 2, there is nothing wrong with asking the Lord to heal you from cancer, whether you are in the midst of treatment, in your first year of surveillance, or ten years after being cancer free. Persistence and perseverance with regard to cancer healing are not sinful. God is listening, and He is more than able to heal you from cancer. Do not question His ability to heal, but trust in His perfect plan for your life.

> Do not question His ability to heal, but trust in His perfect plan for your life.

Despite his repeated request, Paul's affliction was not removed. Paul recognized that the presence of the "thorn" was the best way for God to work in his life. In fact, Paul felt his affliction was not removed because he might become conceited. In Paul's ministry, the purpose of his trial and the presence of a "thorn" seemed sensible. Paul had a close relationship with Christ and might have been prone to pride when it came to spreading the Gospel to the Gentiles. Conceit would give glory and honor to Paul, rather than Christ. We know the purpose behind Paul's "thorn," but what might be the reason for your cancer? The reason for your cancer may not be as easily apparent as the reason for Paul's thorn, but rest assured, you are not going through this in vain. Even if you cannot pinpoint the particular reason, as Paul was able to, the presence of cancer is one way for God to work in your life. The cancer journey is for your good and His glory (recall Romans 8:28).

The most important lesson we can learn from Paul's "thorn" is that Paul knew Christ's grace was sufficient to sustain him. Grace is that powerful, life-changing word that means an unmerited gift freely given. MacArthur further describes grace as "a dynamic force, a dynamic and benevolent power that applies the goodness of God and the resources of God to our lives to save us, to keep us, to enable us, to deliver us, to sanctify us, to glorify us. All of God's good favors to

His children are given through the means of this benevolent goodness called grace."[25]

Not only did Christ give Paul grace through his trial, but He gave Paul a *sufficient* amount of grace—not just a small amount, but a sufficient amount—and, I would argue, the perfect amount. Sufficient means enough. Paul did not need to be healed. He simply needed a "sufficient" amount of Christ's grace to sustain him. The Lord's grace is sufficient in times of weakness or hardship. His grace is sufficient in times of sickness and pain. His grace is sufficient in times of fear and uncertainty. His grace is sufficient in times of loneliness and sorrow.

Not only is His grace sufficient, but the Lord showcases His mercy and power through those who are weak and totally dependent upon Him. Consider Paul's statement, "If I must boast, I will boast of the things that show my weakness" (2 Corinthians 11:30). There are many other examples of this. Moses did not have the gift of speaking, yet the Lord used him to confront Pharaoh on behalf of the Israelites enslaved in Egypt. Gideon went to battle with only 300 men because the Lord did not want the Israelites to boast in their own victory, but to recognize that

> Not only is His grace sufficient, but the Lord showcases His mercy and power through those who are weak and totally dependent upon Him.

the Lord won the battle for them (Judges 7). Even the much hoped for Messiah did not come as a powerful king or warrior. Christ came as a helpless baby.

Other heroes of faith have also proven this principle. Some might consider blindness a weakness and a thorn, but Francis Jane Crosby did not. Fanny Crosby was not born blind. She became blind when she was only two months old. Despite her blindness, she composed many popular hymns like "Blessed Assurance" and "Safe in the Arms of Jesus." The Lord used her weakness to compose many of our beloved hymns. She was content with her ailment, in her own words, "Because when I get to heaven, the first face that shall ever gladden my sight will be that of my Savior."[26]

Have you completed all your cancer treatment and now live in the unknown world of surveillance? Do you dread the thought of your oncologist telling you that your cancer has recurred? Or, perhaps, you have an advanced cancer that has already recurred? Is cancer a "thorn" in your flesh? Whether God chooses to heal you or not has nothing to do with the amount of love and grace He has for you. He gives

> Your identity rests in your relationship with God and how you choose to live your daily life.

more grace than we could ever deserve, and His love for us is more than we can comprehend. Remember, cancer does not define you.

Your identity rests in your relationship with God and how you choose to live your daily life. "And after you have suffered a little while, the God of all grace, who has called you to His eternal glory in Christ, will Himself restore, confirm, strengthen, and establish you" (1 Peter 5:10).

Your ministry through the cancer journey does not stop during the surveillance process. Whether the Lord cures you or chooses to keep cancer as part of your life, there is a purpose for your cancer. Part of your journey may be discovering why the Lord has chosen you for this task. No matter what calamity you experience, the strength of the Lord will sustain you. Ask Him to give you grace when you fear the return of cancer. Ask Him to give you grace when He will not give you healing. His grace is sufficient to cover all your needs. "He gives power to the faint, and to him who has no might He increases strength. Even youths shall faint and be weary, and young men shall fall exhausted; but they who wait for the Lord shall renew their strength; they shall mount up with wings like eagles; they shall run and not be weary; they shall walk and not faint" (Isaiah 40:29-31).

Paul found contentment in his affliction. To be content means to be perfectly satisfied in the present situation of your life. With His sufficient grace, you will be able to find contentment in God's perfect plan. Don't just rest in the contentment of your "thorn." Boast in your weakness, as Paul did. By boasting in your weakness, you are boasting in the Lord. You are announcing your full trust and faith in Him and all He is doing. As Paul stated in his letter to the Philippians, "...I have *learned* in whatever situation I am to be content. I know how to be brought low, and I know how to abound. In any and every circumstance, I have learned the secret of facing plenty and hunger, abundance and need. I can do all things through Him who strengthens me" (4:11-13, emphasis added). If you have not memorized verse thirteen, then I encourage you to do so right now. The source of your strength is Christ, and small things like cancer do not hinder Him.

# CHAPTER SEVEN

# FINDING COURAGE
# IN THE CONQUEROR

Elizabeth had just received the news. Her breast cancer had progressed. She was only 50 years old, and her second trial of chemotherapy had failed. The PET/CT scan showed growth of the cancer in her liver. What now? She had a family to care for at home, and overall, she didn't feel too bad. There was plenty of fighting left for her to do. When her doctor presented a clinical trial opportunity, she became relieved. There was something else out there—something new to try. Perhaps this would be the right medication.

## THE ROLE OF CLINICAL TRIALS IN CANCER

You may have heard of clinical trials advertised on the radio, where the participant is asked to call a specific number to find out if he qualifies for participation. Participants who are accepted and complete the trial usually earn some sort of monetary benefit. These types of trials are common in large cities where academic institutions reside, but they usually only involve a questionnaire or simple observation of a drug the individual may already be taking. Trials studying cancer therapies are much more complex. There are many misconceptions about clinical trials, so allow me to define what a clinical trial is and why they are so important.

## HOW DO I FIND OUT WHAT CLINICAL TRIALS EXIST?

The best place to look for clinical trials is to first ask your doctor. Most physicians are aware of institutions or colleagues who are performing clinical trials. Academic research institutions and big cities are often places that will have a large number of clinical trials available, but sometimes smaller practices can work in conjunction with these institutions to bring the trials to the smaller communities. The FDA website is also a good resource for clinical trials, and clinicaltrials.gov has a list of current trials available in both the US and other countries.

The Food and Drug Administration (FDA) is the government agency that is "responsible for protecting the public health by assuring the safety, efficacy and security of human and veterinary drugs, biological products, medical devices, our nation's food supply, cosmetics, and products that emit radiation."[27] The FDA controls all pharmaceutical agents—both prescription and over-the-counter medications—present in our market. This does not include alternative therapies or complementary medicine, which we will discuss later in this chapter. When a pharmaceutical company designs a new drug, it must first go through rigorous clinical testing before it can be manufactured and marketed in the United States.

There are four phases of drug testing. Phase 1 clinical trials test the drug in a small group (usually 20-80 people) to determine drug safety and dosage. The effectiveness of the drug is important, but it is generally not the focus of this phase. If the drug appears to be safe and well-tolerated among a small group, then the drug will move into a Phase 2 trial.

The purpose of Phase 2 trials is to give the drug to a larger group (usually 100-300 people) and to test for both safety and efficacy, though again, safety is the top priority. If the drug appears to be safe in this group, and shows signs of effectiveness, then it will move into a Phase 3 study.

Phase 3 studies require many participants (usually 1000-3000) because increasing the number of participants will give better statistical information. Though safety is always a priority, this phase is meant to confirm the efficacy of the medication and give more data as to certain side effects the participants are experiencing. If the data proves to be positive and safe, then the drug will likely be approved by the FDA. Very few drugs actually ever make it to this level. Once approved by the FDA, the drug can then be marketed and manufactured. The newly approved drug will then go through Phase 4 studies, also called post-marketing studies, which are meant to give additional information and guidance for use of the drug in optimal settings.

In America, entrance into a clinical trial is voluntary. Information about the purpose of the trial and the type of treatment being given is provided in great detail to the subjects. Most trials will have specific criteria that the patient must meet in order to qualify. This is to keep the patient population similar so that the statistical data collected can be analyzed appropriately. Once a patient qualifies for the clinical trial, he must sign consent and agree to the specific schedule and testing established by the trial. Very few cancer trials offer a monetary reward to patients for completion, though in certain trials, medications, labs, and procedures may be covered. The physician group or office may receive monetary compensation to cover their incurred expenses, such as staffing, drugs, and supplies. If, at any time, a subject wishes to stop participating in the clinical trial, he or she may do so simply by withdrawing consent.

Throughout the duration of the trial, many checks and balances must be met to ensure the trial is being carried out safely. This will be done by a research coordinator who collects data, the physician who oversees the trial, and outside monitors who periodically check the data that is being submitted. Does this mean the drug is safe? Not necessarily. Much like any medication you see on the market, these drugs will have side effects, and some of those side effects could cause permanent damage or death. If these issues are discovered during the trial, then the trial may be discontinued early.

Probably one of the most important things to consider about clinical trials is the goal of the trial. Most cancer trials test for survival, meaning they look for which drug produces the longest survival in a particular study participant. Often, this means comparing a new drug with the standard of care. If you recall from Chapter 2, the standard of care means the particular agent or treatment modality that seems to provide the best outcome to the most people. If the new drug produces a statistically significant increase in overall survival and is relatively safe, then the trial will likely be successful, and the drug will be approved.

The data collection from a clinical trial takes many years to process; therefore, it takes many years for a new drug to receive FDA approval. According to The Pharmaceutical Research and Manufacturers of America (PhRMA), on average, it takes approximately ten to fifteen years from the time of drug origination to drug approval.[28] As we all know, time is money. Clinical trials cost pharmaceutical companies millions of dollars each year, and at the end of the long process, their drug may not reach approval. If the drug does not get approved, then there is no hope of income from the new medication to cover the cost of the clinical trial. Still, this rigorous process allows us to have the safest, and most effective, drugs available on the market.

Due to the lengthy time it takes for a drug to be approved and the concerns for safety, I have often heard people say that they do not want to participate in a clinical trial because it will not benefit them. On the contrary, participating in a clinical trial gives you access to the latest pharmaceutical technology. Certainly, not all trials will be successful, which is a risk, but history has shown some drugs to be quite effective in the cancers they treat. Even the drugs that are declared the standard of care did not get in that position without first going through the clinical trial process.

A SUCCESS STORY

Allow me to give you an example of a cancer "miracle" drug. Gleevec is an oral medication used to treat chronic myelogenous leukemia (CML), which is a form of cancer that affects a certain type of white blood cell. The key characteristic of CML, and the connection it has with Gleevec, is a chromosome abnormality of chromosomes 9 and 22 (recall our discussion on chromosomes from Chapter 1). In this disease, a piece of chromosome 22 is transferred to chromosome 9, causing it to function abnormally.

On chromosome 9, there is a gene called the "abl" that joins up with a gene on chromosome 22 called the "bcr." Together the "bcr-abl" connection begins to function abnormally, causing an overproduction of immature white cells. Gleevec, originally called ST1571, was developed in the early 1990s as an inhibitor of the "bcr-abl" gene, thus inhibiting the excessive production of abnormal white cells.[29] The drug was successful because it was both safe and effective. In the Phase 1 clinical trials, the drug had a 98 to nearly 100% response rate. Most Phase 1 clinical trials are considered successful if they have a 20% response rate.

The drug continued to move through the phases of clinical trials, showing similar response rates and an excellent safety profile. In 2001, Gleevec was approved by the FDA. It took ten years from the early stages of development for the drug to gain approval from the FDA. Only those patients who participated in the clinical trial were able to benefit from its early success during the trials. While very few clinical trials exist with this success story, Gleevec is a good example that success can be achieved by participating in clinical trials. Today, even more therapies exist for CML, and the advances of pharmaceuticals in our country are growing at an incredible rate all because of a detailed clinical trial system.

GOOD QUESTIONS TO ASK REGARDING CLINICAL TRIALS:

1. What are the treatment options for my cancer? Are there any clinical trials available for my cancer type?

2. How would the clinical trial be different from the standard of care?

3. Who would be in charge of my care should I qualify for the clinical trial?

4. What additional time or cost would be required for the clinical trial? Do I have to travel somewhere else to receive the treatment?

5. Will my insurance cover the clinical trial, or will the study drug be provided?

6. How will I know if the treatment is working? What will happen if the treatment does not work?

## COMPLEMENTARY AND ALTERNATIVE MEDICINE

The National Center for Complementary and Alternative Medicine defines complementary medicine and alternative medicine as a "group of diverse medical and healthcare systems, practices, and products that are not presently considered to be part of conventional medicine."[30] Conventional medicine is that which is practiced by a licensed medical doctor (M.D.) or a doctor of osteopathy (D.O.), and the treatments are those which have undergone rigorous clinical testing. Complementary and alternative medicines can come in various forms including massage, acupuncture, meditation, energy therapy, herbs, vitamins, or chemicals of an unknown variety. Unfortunately, clinical trials for complementary and alternative medicine are lacking; therefore, their safety and efficacy are unknown.

Patients with cancer are often interested in alternative treatments. When one of these treatments is used in conjunction with conventional therapy, then it is called complementary medicine. For example, adding ginger to the diet to help with nausea from chemotherapy is considered complementary medicine. Alternative medicine is when these treatments are used instead of conventional medicine. For example, in the 1970s, high dose Vitamin C was thought to be

## WHAT IS ENERGY THERAPY? IS ENERGY THERAPY BIBLICAL?

Energy therapy is a form of complementary/alternative medicine used to promote cancer healing and improve quality of life. It is based on the premise that the human body flows with energy and sickness is a loss of balance in that vital energy. Reiki therapy is a specific type of energy therapy from Japanese origins that is administered by "laying on hands." Interestingly, Reiki therapy is not truly Reiki unless it is performed by an individual who has received the Reiki attunement from a Reiki Master.

Reiki therapy is rooted in Buddhism and is, therefore, not a Christian practice. There are some Christians who do practice Reiki and believe that Christ allows us the opportunity to "lay hands" on the afflicted just like He did. This would be a so-called "acceptable" form of utilizing the spiritual gift of healing (1 Corinthians 12:9). However, one must use caution when practicing or participating in energy therapy or Reiki therapy. It is not the act of "laying hands" that is dangerous, but placing hope that the act will heal. Remember, it was not Christ's hands upon the individual that caused healing, but simply the desire and will of the Father through Christ. Recall, Christ was not present when the Centurion's servant was healed and no hands were laid upon him (Matthew 8). I encourage you to use wisdom and discretion when seeking out alternative treatments like Reiki or other forms of energy therapy.

an anti-cancer agent.[31] Many hoped high dose Vitamin C could be used instead of conventional chemotherapy for tumor shrinkage. However, newer trials have proven to be negative and have shown that cancer does not respond to high doses of Vitamin C, whether given orally or intravenously. Today, Vitamin C is used more as a complementary medicine and is being studied in conjunction with conventional treatments in cancers like multiple myeloma.

Before trying any complementary or alternative treatment, you should investigate the treatment. Massage and herbal remedies may be beneficial and therapeutic, but they will not cure the cancer. They are more for symptomatic relief and to help with stress. Internet websites advertising chemicals or vitamins should be used with caution as, often, these sites are simply after your money. Finally, traveling to other countries to receive alternative treatments has become a popular practice. When traveling to other countries, the standard of care and regulations of the FDA no longer apply, so use discernment and be well-informed about the treatment. If you have an oncologist in the US, then it is important to keep them aware of all the medications you are taking.

For more information on complementary and alternative medicine, see http://nccam.nih.gov/. For information on herbs and supplements, visit: http://www.nlm.nih.gov/medlineplus/druginfo/herb_All.html

ENCOURAGEMENT FROM THE WORD

*What then? Only that in every way, whether in pretense or in truth, Christ is proclaimed, and in that I rejoice. Yes, and I will rejoice, for I know that through your prayers and the help of the Spirit of Jesus Christ this will turn out for my deliverance, as it is my eager expectation and hope that I will not be at all ashamed, but that with full courage now as always Christ will be honored in my body, whether by life or by death. For to me to live is Christ, and to die is gain. If I am to live in the flesh, that means fruitful labor for me. Yet which I shall choose I cannot tell. I am hard pressed between the two. My desire is to depart and be with Christ, for that is far better. But to remain in the flesh is more necessary on your account.* (Philippians 1:18-24)

As this passage in Philippians says, "What then?" For the past few chapters, we've established that there is a reason for any trial, including a cancer diagnosis. God makes no mistakes. There has been no promise of the "easy" life as a believer, yet God's purpose for our lives is always good and right. Suffering should not come as a surprise to the believer (1 Peter 4:12). Our job is not to figure out *why* God has brought this trial upon us, but to continue to love and serve Him *through* the trial and to do so with joy. Paul continued to serve God despite the many trials and tribulations he endured, including the thorn in his flesh, as we discussed in Chapter 6.

Now, what do you do with the reality of cancer? What is your purpose for the next hour, day, week, or year? Your purpose is to serve God and to do all things to His glory and honor. 1 Corinthians 10:31 says, "...whatever you do, do all to the glory of God." Paul teaches us how to serve and glorify Christ in his letter to the

> Your purpose is to serve God and to do all things to His glory and honor.

Philippians. In the beginning of this letter, we find Paul writing to the Philippians from jail. Yet this letter is full of encouragement and joy. Paul states his purpose for living—to honor Christ by proclaiming the Gospel and by fruitful labor. He feels like the Lord has called him to minister to the Philippians, and that he will likely be freed from jail so that he can return to them in the future. He further explains that being at home with Christ is far better than continuing to live on earth. In fact, Paul states he would rather be with Christ, but he understands that the Lord has not finished with him and that his earthly duties are not yet complete.

We have the opportunity to adopt the same "mission statement" as Paul. Our purpose in life, no matter the hardship or tribulation we face, should be to honor and glorify Christ by proclaiming the Gospel and by producing fruitful labor. This purpose can be carried out until the Lord takes us home to be with Christ. John Piper, in his book *Don't Waste Your Life,* teaches us to magnify Christ as Paul magnified

Christ. "Whenever something is of tremendous value to you, and you cherish its beauty or power or uniqueness, you want to draw others' attention to it and waken in them the same joy. That is why Paul's all-consuming goal in life was for Christ to be magnified. Christ was of infinite value to Paul, and so Paul longed for others to see and savor this value."[32]

We must proclaim Christ in our daily living—when we wake in the morning and have a quiet time with Him, when we begin our daily tasks to manage our households and work our jobs, and when we encounter others, whether family, friends, or strangers. We can proclaim Christ in the physician's office, infusion room, and support groups. We should proclaim Christ in prayer and in worship. We must also let every job and task we perform be Christ-focused and Christ-centered because He is of infinite value to us, and we want others to see Him through us.

Proclaiming Christ and having fruitful labor during the cancer journey are not easy tasks. Many things can hinder us, especially when we are suffering in a trial. We may find ourselves angry that God would afflict us with cancer. Anger results when we feel as though God has treated us unjustly by afflicting us with disease or hardship. How often we forget the punishment for sin is death and that God, in His mercy, has rescued us by providing redemption through Christ!

Anger is a very powerful emotion, and it will consume and distract you from the ministry Christ calls you to. Another distraction from ministry is fear. Fear of death or fear of the unknown will paralyze you and keep you from pursuing Christ. Fear is a symptom of distrust in Christ. The sister emotions to fear are anxiety and worry. Finally, the realization of human frailty can lead to the silencing of God and the listening to the deafening sounds of self. These types of distractions can cause a rampant plague of doubt in your heart and will not only keep you from ministry, but also separate you from Christ.

How do we overcome these obstacles so that we can continue to proclaim Christ and have fruitful labor? In his book, *Holiness*, J.C. Ryle describes true Christian living as a battle. This warfare is against the flesh, the world, and the devil. It is a fight that requires faith in Christ, and that faith will require courage. Nothing gives us more courage for accomplishing the Lord's work than looking to Christ and trusting in Him. He is the ultimate Conqueror for proclaiming the Gospel and the perfect example of fruitful labor. He is the conqueror of sin, the conqueror in the battle of good and evil, and the conqueror for His chosen people. He is the

> Nothing gives us more courage for accomplishing the Lord's work than looking to Christ and trusting in Him.

perfect friend (John 15:15) and the perfect servant (John 13:1-17). As Ryle describes, He is "a mighty Savior, an interceding Savior, a sympathizing Savior,"[33] and because of what Christ has done, we too are conquerors.

In fact, Romans 8 says, "we are more than conquerors through Him who loved us. For I am sure that neither death nor life, nor angels nor rulers, nor things present nor things to come, nor powers, nor height nor depth, nor anything else in all creation, will be able to separate us from the love of God in Christ Jesus our Lord" (Romans 8:37-39). Being a conqueror with Christ means nothing can separate us from Him (verse 35), not even cancer. If we cannot be separated from Him, then we can have courage in all that He will accomplish through us.

Courage was not foreign to Paul. While Paul was imprisoned in Acts 23, the Lord told him to have courage because his ministry would continue. "'Take courage, for as you have testified to the facts about Me in Jerusalem, so you must testify also in Rome'" (Acts 23:11). Paul would not die in Jerusalem, but he would stand trial in Rome, and during that time he would be able to preach and teach the Word of God to the churches. The Lord gave Paul courage, so Paul gives courage to those he ministers to. In his letter, Paul encourages the Philippians to have courage when facing adversaries and suffering. Specifically, Paul wants to see that they "are standing firm in one spirit, with one mind striving side by side for the faith of the Gospel, and not frightened in anything" (Philippians 1:27-28). Did you catch the verbs in this passage? Paul wants the Philippians to stand firm, strive, and to overcome fear. All of these actions will require courage.

The Israelites knew all about adversaries when they were moving into the Promised Land after being slaves in Egypt. The Promised Land was filled with many nations that had to be removed. On multiple occasions, the Lord commanded Joshua and the people to have courage. "Be strong and courageous. Do not fear or be in dread of them, for it is the Lord your God who goes with you. He will not leave you or forsake you" (Deuteronomy 31:6). They were not to have courage in their own abilities; rather, they were to have courage because they had the Lord on their side. When the Israelites were outnumbered, or when the tasks seemed impossible, the Lord was there to fight the battle for them and give them victory over their enemies.

However, when the Israelites were disobedient and did not keep His commands, the Lord gave them up in battle and caused them to fail. We too must be obedient and follow God's commands. No, we are not subject to the civil laws or ceremonial laws laid out in Exodus, Leviticus, and Deuteronomy, as the Israelites were, but we are subject to moral commands given to us by Christ. "You shall love the Lord your God with all your heart and with all your soul and with all your strength and with all your mind, and your neighbor as yourself" (Luke 10:27). We will fail in our attempts to proclaim Christ and produce fruitful labor if we fail to love God and love others.

We must also have courage when we are suffering. Suffering can come in many forms, such as the persecution that Paul faced or the pain from death and disease that Job faced. Regardless of the origin of suffering, the Bible promises that the testing of our faith through suffering will result in glorifying Christ. Whether by "pruning" the branch (John 15:1-11) to produce good fruit or "refining" gold to make it pure, our suffering is for our good from a God who cares for us. "In this you rejoice, though now for a little while, if necessary, you have been grieved by various trials, so that the tested genuineness of your faith—more precious than gold that perishes though it is tested by fire—may be found to result in praise and glory and honor at the revelation of Jesus Christ" (1 Peter 1:6-7).

Allow me to give you a few words of caution. Courage is necessary for Christ's path and for the work He requests of us. After all, He did tell us to take up our crosses and follow Him (Mark 8:34). However, our work does not bring us salvation in Christ. That gift was given freely when Christ died on the cross. As we mentioned previously, He is the ultimate conqueror over sin and death. We will not find any hope in our works; rather, we serve simply as a result of the work He has done in us. Your faith must be firmly established in Him before you can proclaim the Gospel and produce good fruit.

Another warning when working for Christ: Our work can never take the place of our worship. When Christ came to the house of Mary and Martha in Luke 10, He rebuked Martha for working instead of sitting at His feet worshipping, as Mary was doing. Martha's hospitality was not bad. We are all called to be hospitable. "Do not neglect to show hospitality to strangers, for thereby some have entertained angels unawares" (Hebrews 13:2). Christ, however, was no stranger to this family, and His time on earth was limited. Mary chose to sit at His feet and worship. She chose "the good portion" (Luke 10:42). Yes, there is a time to serve, and we will spend our entire lives serving our brothers and those in need, but more importantly, we must always be willing to worship our Lord. "At the name of Jesus every knee should bow, in heaven and on earth and under the earth, and every tongue confess that Jesus Christ is Lord, to the glory of God the Father" (Philippians 2:10-11).

Are you lacking in courage with your cancer battle? Is it difficult to proclaim the Gospel and produce good fruit during your illness? Perhaps you are asking the same question to God as Elisha's servant asked when they were surrounded by an army of horses and chariots. "Alas, my master! What shall we do?" (2 Kings 6:15). Put your trust in the Almighty God who will come to battle with you. Elisha informed his servant, "'Do not be afraid, for those who are with us are more than those who are with them.' Then Elisha prayed and said, 'O Lord, please open his eyes that he may see.' So the Lord opened the eyes of the young man, and he saw, and behold, the mountain was full of horses and chariots of fire all around Elisha" (2 Kings 6:16-17). Open your eyes. You are never alone. You will never battle cancer alone, and you will never do God's work alone. He is with you

> You are never alone. You will never battle cancer alone, and you will never do God's work alone.

now. He will be with you through the end of your earthly life, and He will be with you through all eternity.

# CHAPTER EIGHT

# FINDING NOURISHMENT
# IN THE BREAD OF LIFE

S am was back for follow-up during his second line of chemotherapy. Unfortunately, the first round of chemotherapy did not put his lymphoma into remission. He was naturally disappointed, and obviously a little concerned. His wife joined him at one of our follow-up appointments. She was also quite concerned to see her husband losing weight so rapidly. The chemotherapy was not causing nausea, vomiting, or diarrhea. He did not have mouth sores, either. After further questioning, he simply said, "I just don't have an appetite."

## WHAT THIS CHAPTER IS NOT ABOUT

Entire books have been written on nutrition and cancer. Most of them are written by a registered dietitian or someone with a PhD degree. Some of these books will go into tremendous detail on the science behind nutrition, like simple carbohydrates versus complex carbohydrates and soluble fiber versus insoluble fiber. Others will explain how to prevent cancer by eating the "right" diet, like a diet high in fiber to prevent colon cancer. Some books may even go into more controversial topics such as organic versus inorganic foods and the so-called "alkaline" diet. This chapter will do none of these things.

In this chapter, I will give you some basic nutritional information and some tips on how to manage weight loss in the cancer setting. This information will be helpful for healthy eating during treatment and for managing mild to moderate weight loss. When the situation turns into severe weight loss and malnutrition, then I refer to a registered dietitian. Fortunately, I have been surrounded by many skilled dietitians in my line of work, and I think they are a wonderful resource for any cancer patient. If you have a dietitian available to you, then by all means, use him or her.

FOOD FOR THOUGHT

If we return to our simple cell discussion from Chapter 1, before it became a cancer cell, then we will find that our cell requires food. Food allows the cell to have energy for the tasks it must perform. There are three basic food groups for a cell: sugar (also known as carbohydrates), proteins (or amino acids), and fats (also known as fatty acids). If we start with the food while it is sitting on our plate and trace it from beginning to end, then we will be able to see how one particular cell gets enough nutrition to perform the task it was designed to do. Your microscopic cells will not do well with undigested food, so the body must break the food down into manageable portions for the cell.

## IS IT TRUE THAT I CANNOT EAT FRESH FRUITS OR VEGETABLES DURING MY CHEMOTHERAPY?

There are two different schools of thought on the subject of fresh fruits and vegetables. Since fruits and vegetables harbor natural bacteria from the soil, then it has been suggested that patients with low white blood cells should avoid these foods to prevent infection from the bacteria. Alternatively, fruits and vegetables are a wonderful source of vitamins and minerals that are necessary for cancer fighting and immunity in the body. A few small studies have been published that said there is no additional risk in those patients who ate fresh fruits and vegetables versus those who avoided them during their treatment.[37, 38] Most physicians now encourage fruits and vegetables with a thick peel and appropriate washing of all fruits and vegetables before consuming.

For dinner tonight, you decide to have grilled chicken, baked potato, and a vegetable medley of broccoli and carrots. Before you even place a bite of food in your mouth, the actual thought of food begins to stimulate some digestive processes in your mouth. The mouth produces enzymes that will help break some of the food down. Once the food enters the mouth, the teeth do a very important job of taking bite-size pieces and breaking them into smaller pieces. The saliva starts to work on that food to aid in the breakdown process. Then you swallow.

The food travels down the esophagus into the stomach, where acids secreted in the stomach further process the food and kill any bacteria that might be present. The food sits in the stomach for a few minutes and, in small increments, it is pushed into the small intestine. By the time the food reaches the small intestine, it has been broken down into simple molecules that can be absorbed by the cells. The grilled chicken and vegetables have been broken down into small proteins and amino acids (which are the building blocks of proteins). The baked potato has been broken down into simple sugars instead of a long, complex sugar. And, if you put butter and sour cream on that baked potato, then those have been broken down into small fat molecules and fatty acids.

Though most of our discussion takes place in the small intestine, we don't want to stop our story at this point. As the food moves though the intestine, it will be absorbed. The digestive system has a remarkable way of keeping everything moving through a series of waves called peristalsis. So the food in the small intestine does not stay there indefinitely. Eventually, it will be dumped into the large intestine. The main goal of the large intestine is to reabsorb water. Very little food will be absorbed in this part of the intestines, but the large intestine is very important in preventing dehydration. At the end of the entire process, the remains will be excreted by the body in the form of stool.

Now that you have glanced at the entire nutritional process, let us re-visit the small intestine, where our food absorption takes place. Some small sugars, proteins/amino acids, and fatty acids have been absorbed. Since the intestinal waves keep everything moving, there is food that will not be absorbed. This will usually be the more complex foods that could not be broken down fast enough. Once absorbed, cells will then take each small molecule through a series of steps to convert these molecules into energy. As with any process, some energy will be expended to make more energy. Sugar, proteins, and fats all go through different processes and make different amounts of energy. Let me assure you that this is one of the most efficient processes ever designed. There can be no doubt that our God is a marvelous engineer.

Fatty acids provide the most energy to the body, but they can also be used for other functions. They are important in the formation of cell structures/membranes and for the formation of important hormones in the body. Cholesterol is a fat compound that has gotten a very bad reputation, but it is an important molecule when the proper quantities are consumed. Unfortunately, fats provide the least amount of satiety to the body, which basically means they are not very filling. Once the fatty acids have been absorbed and converted into the energy necessary, or are utilized as a necessary tool in the body, the leftover fatty acids will be stored in the form of adipose tissue (or fat tissue).

Proteins, or amino acids, provide the least amount of energy to the body, but they can still be used for energy if necessary. Their main purpose is to be building blocks for muscle and for tissue repair. There are twenty amino acids in the body. Our bodies have the capability of making eleven of them, but we must take in the other nine through our diet. These nine are called essential amino acids because they must be absorbed from the food we eat. When protein needs are not met, the body will become malnourished and will break down muscles to get the necessary amino acids to make energy. Proteins do provide the most satiety in the diet, which means we feel the most full when we consume protein. Excess amino acids are converted into storage if they are not used. This could be in the form of adipose tissue, just as in the case of fatty acids.

Carbohydrates, or sugars, are the third nutrient for the body and are considered the principal energy source. Their main purpose is to provide energy for the body, rather than to be used as a tool, like proteins and fats. Sugar molecules come in all different sizes and must therefore be broken down to a simple sugar, such as glucose, before the body can use them. But sugar is not the only component of the carbohydrate class. Fiber is indigestible plant material that is categorized as a carbohydrate as well. When fiber is mixed in with the food trying to be absorbed, then it causes a delay in the absorption of simple sugars and fatty acids. On our scale of fullness, carbohydrates rank right in the middle, though fiber does increase satiety and help you feel full.

Hopefully, from this discussion, you can see how important each of these nutrients is to the body, and that each one has a place and purpose in its normal functioning. Eliminating one of these basic groups can be detrimental for the body, but an abundance of one particular group can also be dangerous. There is one more category that is important to our daily function. The broccoli and carrots on our dinner plate contain more than just amino acids and fiber. Vitamins and minerals are also essential to our survival. They do not provide any energy for us, but they are

## ARE THERE ANY MEDICATIONS I CAN TAKE TO BOOST MY APPETITE?

There are several pharmaceutical medications now available to boost appetite. Megestrol is typically the first line medication for appetite stimulation. It is relatively inexpensive because it comes in generic form. Marinol, or dronabinol, is a more expensive medication. However, in addition to increasing appetite, Marinol also works well to decrease nausea. Finally, some medications, like Remeron, are used for depression and have an associated side effect of increasing appetite. As with any medication, side effects are likely and will vary based on the individual.

necessary to the daily processes that the various cells must perform. For example, Vitamin A is important for our vision, while Vitamin C helps combat disease. Vitamin D promotes the absorption of calcium (a mineral), which is essential to bone health.

## CAN FOOD ACTUALLY CAUSE CANCER?

Very seldom does a day go by without a national news station or local paper quoting some new study implicating a certain food causing cancer. Milk, for example—a seemingly healthy part of any diet for its calcium—has been implicated in causing cancer. Is it the saturated fat present in milk, or is it the hormones given to the cow to aid in milk production, or is it the antibiotics given to the cow to prevent infection? Foods that have gotten more press lately for their healthy qualities are also subject to accusations of cancer. For example, eating fish is considered to be healthy because omega-3 fatty acids are good for cognitive development and a healthy heart. Yet, fish contain polychlorinated biphenyls (PCBs), which are toxic in large quantities. But do fish actually have large enough quantities to do harm? If the debate isn't clear with these two examples, then please allow one more. Soy is a very hot topic now because of the health benefits. Soybeans are high in protein and are loaded with minerals. They protect against both heart disease and cancer and have many other beneficial health properties, such as minimizing hot flashes in menopause and preventing bone loss. But could too much soy be harmful? Soy has a chemical composition similar to estrogen—hence, why it is beneficial in menopause and osteoporosis—but you may recall that too much estrogen is harmful in women at risk for breast cancer.

These three examples are not meant to scare you or to deter you from the media, and it is doubtful that these foods actually cause cancer. I simply want to present some of the ongoing debates. If you decide to limit your farmed fish consumption or switch from cow's milk to soy milk, then by all means, do what you think is best with the data that is available. The conclusion I have come to with the many articles and study publications I have read is that a well-balanced diet rich in fruits and vegetables with lean meats and whole grains is probably the healthiest diet available.

The benefits of a healthy diet generally outweigh any harm that could be present in certain "harmful" foods that are often not consumed in harmful quantities, anyway. This same principle applies for foods that are sprayed with pesticides versus those that are grown in a certified organic field. Of course, I'm sure a few eyebrows were raised with this statement, but again, eating foods that have been sprayed with pesticides is not the same as drinking a bottle of dichlorodiphenyltrichloroethane, a.k.a. DDT (which by the way is no longer used in the US), just like eating a few farmed-raised fish is not the same as drinking a bottle of PCB. We must all choose our battles.

BUT SUGAR FEEDS THE CANCER...

If there is a particular diet/food out there that is known to cure cancer or directly cause cancer, then we would all adjust our diet to indulge in the cure and eliminate the cause. However, at this time, there is no scientific evidence pointing to one particular nutritional cure or cause of cancer. There are many nutritional benefits from a well-balanced diet. This includes carbohydrate intake. Probably the most common dietary question I receive from patients is, "Should I avoid sugar since it will feed the cancer?" The origin of this question comes from Otto Warburg, a Nobel Peace Prize winner in 1927, who researched the origin of tumors and concluded that the origin of cancer was due to mitochondrial dysfunction, and that tumor cells survived on oxygen and fermentation of glucose.[34]

Though brilliant in his time, we now know more about tumor origination because we now understand DNA and the role it plays in cell life. Recall our discussion in Chapter 1. Cancer begins when a single cell's DNA develops a mistake and that mistake is copied many times over, creating thousands of dysfunctional cells. But the origination of cancer as a DNA problem still does not address the plausible theory that sugar feeds cancer. After all, cancer cells are just cells that survive on the major energy source of glucose. In his paper, "The Metabolism of Tumors in the Body," Warburg draws the conclusion that glucose accelerates tumor growth.[35] However, these experiments were done "in vitro" and, therefore, do not take into account the actions of other organs—particularly the liver, when glucose is depleted.

When deprived of glucose, the body is capable of making glucose through a process called gluconeogenesis. This process is carried out primarily by the liver and requires protein and fatty acids to be converted into glucose. Thus, it is practically impossible to starve the body of sugar. As emphasized previously, probably the best diet for both cancer prevention and cancer fighting is a well-balanced diet. More so, "the most convincing evidence for the cancer-fighting potential of diet supports a high total intake of fruits and vegetables."[36]

## THE ROLE OF SUPPLEMENTS

To help her husband with his declining appetite and weight loss, Sam's wife went to the store to buy him some supplements. When she walked down the aisle where they were located, she was overwhelmed at the many different products—extra protein, low sugar, more calories, name brand versus generic, etc. She called me right away to find out what would be the best for him.

Weight loss is a huge concern for cancer patients and medical providers, and it is a sign that the body is using more energy (in the form of calories) than it is consuming. Think of your body as an ATM machine. The more food (calories) you put into the body, the bigger your "bank account" will be and the more calories/energy the body must utilize to maintain a balanced weight. If the body does not utilize the calories, then it will store the excess in the form of fat. Obesity in the United States is rampant because more people are "depositing" to their ATM machine and fattening their bank account (which is great when speaking monetarily, but not great when speaking about weight). Weight loss, however, occurs in cancer patients because the amount of calories the body consumes is not enough to keep up with the demands of the body. Because of the

---

## I AM TRYING TO DRINK SUPPLEMENTS, BUT THEY DO NOT TASTE GOOD. WHAT CAN I DO?

This is a very common question. The best answer is: Get creative. What types of food do you like? If you love peaches, try blending some peaches with your favorite supplement. Most fruits are easily combined with the supplement to make a smoothie. Ice cream is also a great way to make the supplement taste better, but be careful of the additional sugar that ice cream will add. Adding a flavored yogurt will not only improve the taste, but it will add some of those "good bacteria" (probiotics) to your diet. You can even get creative with various extracts and liquors. Adding mint extract to your favorite chocolate supplement is sure to improve the taste. There are also many websites and cookbooks available for cancer patients with great recipes.

exponential growth rate of cancer cells, the body will require more calories to function adequately. While it sounds like a good idea to "starve" the cancer, this will not work. Starving the cancer will cause the body to break down important tissues in the body, like muscle, to get the adequate amount of calories for functioning.

When choosing a supplement, it is important to look at the nutritional content listed on the side. Most supplements are tailored to meet basic nutritional needs. In general, choose a supplement high in calories and protein. Calories are important in providing much needed energy for the body's normal activities, and protein will help maintain muscle mass. Other supplements are more patient-specific. For example, Glucerna has fewer carbohydrates and is therefore better for diabetics. High fiber supplements are also available. Many big chain grocery stores or pharmacies will have their own brand of supplements that are comparable to supplements like Boost or Ensure, and they will be less expensive. Also, buying at wholesale clubs may save you money.

Finally, some supplements are made with soy, while others are milk-based (which means they contain lactose). If you are sensitive to lactose, then milk-based supplements will likely cause upset stomach and gas. As a caution, supplements can sometimes cause diarrhea, but this does not mean that you are lactose intolerant. In some patients, the high nutritional content—specifically the carbohydrates—can draw water into the intestines. This additional water then causes the patient to experience diarrhea. To avoid diarrhea, supplements are best used as "supplements," rather than as full meal replacement. It is important to eat small, frequent meals throughout the day.

## WHEN TO SEE A DIETITIAN

There are many cancer patients who would benefit from the expertise of a dietician, especially since a physician has only a limited amount of time for each office visit. There are some cancer diagnoses that warrant the aid of a dietician from the very beginning. Head and neck cancer, esophageal cancer, and gastric cancer will affect a patient's nutritional status and weight. Having a dietary consult from the beginning can prevent some of the drastic malnutrition and weight loss that can result from these cancers and their treatments. Dieticians can also be quite useful when cancer patients receiving treatment also have diabetes or an underlying intestinal disease, such as Crohn's disease or celiac disease. Finally, dieticians are a great resource for patients who have a feeding tube or those who are receiving parenteral feedings (where all nutritional needs are met intravenously instead of utilizing the stomach/intestines for digestion).

ENCOURAGEMENT FROM THE WORD

*I led them with cords of kindness, with the bands of love, and I became to them as one who eases the yoke on their jaws, and I bent down to them and fed them.* (Hosea 11:4)

Evelyn had been in the hospital for five days and was doing better. She was receiving IV antibiotics after developing a serious infection. Her white blood cells had been very low after her chemotherapy, but they were starting to recover. She would probably go home in the next few days. One particular morning, while I was doing my hospital rounds, I asked her if there was anything she needed to make her more comfortable. She picked up her Bible from the table and told me she had lost her reading glasses. She asked me if I could help her locate a new pair so that she could resume her daily Bible reading. In this chapter we have "fed" our bodies with the nutrients required to make energy for daily living. Now we must discuss the nutrients our soul needs for our spiritual living. The proper diet for our soul is the Bread of Life, Jesus Christ (John 6:35).

The Scripture is filled with food as a sign of God's provision and as a symbol for spiritual nourishment. The Israelites depended on manna from heaven each day while they were migrating to the Promised Land. They were instructed to gather only what was needed for the day, and they could gather twice as much in preparation for the Sabbath. Daniel and his three friends asked to eat a diet of vegetables when they were taken into King Nebuchadnezzar's palace so they would not defile themselves with the King's food. "At the end of ten days it was seen that they were better in appearance and fatter in flesh than all the youths who ate the king's food. So the steward took away their food and the wine they were to drink, and gave them vegetables" (Daniel 1:15-16). In the New Testament, we find Christ providing bread and fish for the crowd of five thousand people, with several baskets of leftovers. More importantly, the elements for the Lord's Table are symbols of the sacrifice of Christ in His death.

In John 6, Jesus, the Divine Dietician, gives a lesson in nutrition to His disciples and to the crowd so earnestly seeking Him. After feeding five thousand people with only five loaves and two fish, Christ withdrew from the crowd to find solitude while His disciples traveled by boat across the sea to Capernaum. The next day, the crowd was again looking for Christ. They were seeking Him because their bellies were filled, and they were satisfied physically. Jesus, however, wanted to satisfy them spiritually. He wanted to give them the spiritual nourishment that comes from God the Father. He wanted to give them Himself. Deuteronomy 8:3 says, "Man does not live by bread alone, but man lives by every word that comes from the mouth of the Lord."

How can we be spiritually nourished? The crowd thought their spiritual food must be earned much like a laborer goes out each day to earn his wages. Professor and Theologian, J. Dwight Pentecost, further describes the crowd's erroneous views. "According to the Pharisaic tradition, one entered the kingdom by works consisting of observing the traditions of the Pharisees."[39] Even modern Christianity is often mistaken as a "works based" religion. Yet Christ tells the crowd that eternal life is found through belief in the One sent by God. Eternal life is found by believing in Christ. "Whoever believes in the Son has eternal life; whoever does not obey the Son shall not see life, but the wrath of God remains on him" (John 3:36).

Dear friend, the first step for a spiritual diet is redemption through Christ. And redemption cannot be accomplished without belief in Christ. Praise God if you have believed! But, let us not be mistaken at how difficult it is to believe. It is not only difficult, it is impossible to believe in Christ unless God the Father wills it. Christ explained this impossibility to Nicodemus, "The wind blows where it wishes, and you hear its sound, but you do not know where it comes from or where it goes. So it is with everyone who is born of the Spirit" (John 3:8). Christ also spoke very plainly to the crowd at Capernaum, "...no one can come to Me [Christ] unless it is granted him by the Father" (John 6:65). Your Heavenly Father has to be the

One to give you the ability to believe in Christ. We can do nothing, nor have done anything, on our own merit to earn belief in Christ.

With the ability to believe, our only adequate response should be like that of the father whose son had an unclean spirit, "I believe; help my unbelief!" (Mark 9:24). When you are sitting in the physician's office receiving your treatment, ask your Father, "help my unbelief." When you are at home weary from the chemotherapy or radiation side effects, ask your Father, "help my unbelief." When you are waiting for test results, ask your Father, "help my unbelief." We will never have the perfect amount of faith, but if we will recognize our lack of faith and ask for more, then our Father will supply the faith we need. Our Father delights in giving us good things (Matthew 7:11).

> We will never have the perfect amount of faith, but if we will recognize our lack of faith and ask for more, then our Father will supply the faith we need.

When the father of the boy called out, "Help my unbelief," what he really wanted was a better understanding of who Christ is and what He is capable of doing. What the father really wanted was to increase his knowledge of Christ. Sinclair Ferguson, in his book, *The Christian Life*, says, "All trust is ultimately dependent on knowledge...true knowledge in the Bible invariably involves personal fellowship."[40] If we desire, as the father desired, to have more faith in Christ, then we must increase our knowledge of Him. We must seek after Him with a fervency and passion above any hobby, learned skill, or relationship.

My husband had a vested interest in getting to know me when we were dating. He would ask my college roommate about my likes and dislikes. He would seek to find the things that I enjoyed doing, and he would prepare the foods that I liked to eat. He would spend hours "studying" me. Why? Because he desired to be in a relationship with me and wanted to know everything about me. The same holds true for our relationship with Christ. When we ask Him to "help our unbelief," He will not only increase our faith, but He will also give us the desire to know Him better. The Lord was pleased to grant Solomon wisdom when he asked for it. Without a doubt, the Lord will be pleased to grant us the desire to know Him better. Psalm 42:1 captures the essence of what our desire should be, "As a deer pants for flowing streams, so pants my soul for You, O God."

Not only does Christ give us the desire to know Him, but He also provides the tools for us to know Him. Before we ever became Christians, God revealed Himself to the entire world through creation. "The heavens declare the glory of God, and the sky above proclaims His handiwork" (Psalm 19:1). As believers, now we have the opportunity for a deeper and better understanding of God. The Lord has revealed Himself to us through the Scriptures and through the Holy Spirit.

2 Timothy 3:16-17 says, "All Scripture is breathed out by God and profitable for teaching, for reproof, for correction, and for training in righteousness, that the man of God may be complete, equipped for every good work." When Paul and Silas were in Berea, they preached the Word to the Jews in the synagogue, and the Jews "received the Word with all eagerness, examining the Scriptures daily to see if these things were so" (Acts 17:11). Thankfully, the Scriptures are available to us for our evaluation and examination. We have the same opportunity to increase our knowledge by reading and studying the Scriptures. According to Ferguson, the Scripture "explains to us the pattern of God's purposes, and this give us heart when we go through periods of trial or days of spiritual dryness. It provides us with 'great and precious promises' from God (2 Peter 1:4, NIV) to encourage and assure us as we battle on for Christ."[40]

Yet sometimes, the Scriptures are difficult to understand and confusing. As the eunuch in Acts 8 was guided by Philip, we also have the opportunity to study the Word with fellow believers and learn from each other. Colossians 3:16 tells us to, "Let the Word of Christ dwell in you richly, teaching and admonishing one another in all wisdom, singing psalms and hymns and spiritual songs, with thankfulness in your hearts to God." Do you read the Scriptures daily? Do you seek to memorize and understand the passages? Do you attend a Scripture-based Bible study where you can be with fellow believers? If the Scriptures are not part of your everyday schedule, then your knowledge of God will be limited and your faith will be weak.

We have the opportunity to not only increase our knowledge of Him through the Scriptures, but to also increase our knowledge through the Holy Spirit. How fortunate we are to have the Helper! When Christ was preparing His disciples for His earthly departure, He promised them that the Holy Spirit would come. "But the Helper, the Holy Spirit, whom the Father will send in My name, He will teach you all things and bring to your remembrance all that I have said to you" (John 14:26). A specific aspect of the Holy Spirit's work (and He has many jobs) is to teach us about God. The Holy Spirit also recalls to our minds things we may have forgotten. Have you ever recalled a particular Scripture or has the appropriate Scripture ever been revealed to you at the perfect time—the time when you needed to hear it most? That is the work of the Holy Spirit. How blessed the disciples were to have Christ teach them during His earthly ministry, and we too have that same blessing through the Holy Spirit. 1 Corinthians 2:12-13 says, "Now we have received not the spirit of the world, but the Spirit who is from God, that we might understand the things freely given us by God. And we impart this in words not taught by human wisdom but taught by the Spirit, interpreting spiritual truths to those who are spiritual."

We will never know enough about God. As the Psalmist put it, "Such knowledge is too wonderful for me; it is high; I cannot attain it" (Psalm 139:6). Oh, that we might spend our lives getting to know our God as a young man seeks to know his bride! The more we know about God—His sovereignty, His perfect plan of redemption, His love for His children, His mercies—the more we are able to place our full trust and faith in Him during difficult trials like cancer. When you are in the infusion room, take time to read and study one characteristic of God.[41] Perhaps you need to learn about His goodness. When you are pondering what the outcome of your cancer diagnosis will be, learn about the attributes of God. Perhaps you need to learn about the Lord's omniscience. When you are eating and have that awful metallic taste from the chemotherapy, learn more about the names of God. Perhaps you need to learn more about the Bread of Life. "Jesus said to them, 'I am the bread of life; whoever comes to Me shall not hunger, and whoever believes in Me shall never thirst'" (John 6:35).

> The more we know about God—His sovereignty, His perfect plan of redemption, His love for His children, His mercies—the more we are able to place our full trust and faith in Him during difficult trials like cancer.

# CHAPTER NINE
# FINDING SUPPORT
# FROM THE BODY

The room was crowded. Terry brought her husband, both daughters, and a son-in-law to the visit. After being diagnosed with colon cancer and undergoing several staging studies, this was the visit they had all been anxiously awaiting. This was when the physician would tell her how bad the cancer was, what the treatment options were, and whether or not she would be cured. She was still in shock. Certainly, she needed moral support, but she also needed every set of ears just so she could capture each bit of information her doctor was saying.

## A FAMILY AFFAIR

In the oncology office, there are two major visits that, generally, the entire family attends. The first is when the cancer has been

## I AM RECEIVING CHEMOTHERAPY. IS THERE ANY RISK FOR CHEMOTHERAPY EXPOSURE TO MY FAMILY?

The risk for chemotherapy exposure at home is a two-fold problem. Because chemotherapy delivery can now be in pill form, or some patients may bring a pump home and have chemotherapy infusing over several days, there can be direct exposure with the chemical. Alternatively, once the chemotherapy has been given, it will be present in the body for 24 to 72 hours after delivery. The body must then metabolize the chemotherapy and excrete it through the urine or stool. Therefore, there is also a risk of secondary chemotherapy exposure to family members. To minimize exposure, your family or caregiver should use caution when handling any pills or equipment associated with the chemotherapy. If a spill does occur at home, then call your provider or home health agency to see how best to clean the area. Caregivers should wear gloves when cleaning soiled linens or clothes or when cleaning toilets or basins that have been used recently by someone receiving chemotherapy. If you have small children in the home, then keep all pills out of reach.

recently diagnosed, and the family anxiously hears the plan for treatment and the side effects involved. The second is when the cancer has won the battle and the family must solemnly begin the journey through the final stages of life. Up until now, we have spent most of our discussion on the physical aspects of cancer. In this chapter, we will open up the emotional side of cancer and how it affects you and those closest to you. Cancer might not be such a big deal if it wasn't for the impact that it has on those we love. Family and friends are afraid to lose you, and you are afraid to lose them. I want to emphasize again that not all cancers are terminal, but that doesn't stop you, or your loved ones, from fearing the loss of your life.

There is no set standard for dealing with your spouse, children, or distant family members. The dynamics of a family are as versatile and changing as the waves upon the sea. When it comes to appointments, infusions, or tests, each patient has certain preferences that will vary from one individual to the next. You may desire to have your spouse with you at each visit, or you may desire to come alone. Some patients want a friend to sit with them in chemotherapy, while others would rather sleep or read.

Though your comfort is important, sometimes your wishes are not the only thing to keep in mind. Husbands are often torn between wanting to be with their wives and needing to work to support the family. Adult children often have the same struggles. They want to support their parents, but they may have families of their own that require attention. Wives are natural multi-taskers and will want to take care of additional needs (do the grocery shopping, pick up any medications, etc), while their husbands receive treatment. To avoid feeling guilty and to address the needs of both you and your loved ones, here are a few tips to keep in mind:

1. Have a family meeting so that each person can communicate their desires for your treatment and how

they might be able to best help you. It may be helpful to have a family meeting with your physician so that each person can ask questions and fully understand both the disease and the treatment options.

2.  Once a plan has been made (whether it is a plan for treatment or a plan for comfort), organize a schedule for tasks that can be done, and discuss who will be designated to do the task. For example, a prescription needs to be picked up from the pharmacy. Who will be picking it up?

3.  Be flexible. The schedule will change. Unexpected events will occur. If you are anxious, then the family will feel anxious too.

4.  Do not forget about your church family. Your church will want to walk this journey with you. They will want to pray for you. They will want to serve you—perhaps by giving a few meals each week, perhaps helping you with financial needs, or perhaps sitting with you in the treatment room. It is best to give your church family some parameters on how best they can help you and your family during this difficult time.

5.  Utilize long-distance family members when able. An adult child (or other relative) living a long distance from you may wish to be involved, but they will not be able to

attend each treatment or appointment. When the individual does come, he/she may want to step in to give another family member a break. Also, keeping long-distance family members informed will help ease their anxiety.

## HIPPA

Cancer may be a family affair, but a physician's office will be very careful about what information they give—and to whom. This is not to be rude. It is the law. "The Privacy Rule, a Federal law, gives you rights over your health information and sets rules and limits on who can look at and receive your health information."[42] Medical offices are not

## I WOULD LIKE TO STOP TREATMENT, BUT I THINK MY FAMILY WILL BE UPSET. WHAT SHOULD I DO?

The decision to start or stop treatment is always in the hands of the patient. In situations like these—especially when the family wants their loved one to continue receiving treatment—it is a good idea to get all the options presented and to have a family meeting regarding the decision. It may even be possible to have a family meeting with the physician so that each person can ask their questions and get a clear idea of the options. Good communication is important so that no family member will feel as though they are being left out of the decision making process, or so each person will understand how you as the patient feel and why you are making this particular decision.

allowed to give out your health information to anyone without your permission. This includes a spouse or other family member.

The law, in its most simplistic form, not only prevents a medical office from giving your health information out, but it also requires the medical office to enforce safeguards to protect your information. The law, in a more complicated form, also requires health insurers, government programs like Medicare, and healthcare clearinghouses to protect your information. There are some exceptions to this rule. These include providing necessary information for public health purposes and proper reporting to the police. Also, life insurers, employers, and state agencies are not required to adhere to the law. For more information, visit the HIPPA website: http://www.hhs.gov/ocr/privacy/hipaa/understanding/consumers/index.html.


SUPPORT GROUPS

Paul had been through so much in such a short period of time. He was diagnosed with multiple myeloma and had started chemotherapy. Shortly after his first few treatments, he developed an infection that required hospitalization for intravenous antibiotics. After being discharged, he developed severe diarrhea and had to be readmitted to the hospital for more antibiotics. Was this normal? He desperately wanted to talk with someone who was in the same situation. He wanted to know if this was all "par for the course." His wife suggested a support group but, after looking around, there was not a multiple myeloma support group in the community. At his next appointment in our office, Paul asked if there was another patient who had multiple myeloma with whom he could speak.

It is quite natural, in your cancer journey, to want to compare notes and experiences with someone who is walking the same path as you. Medical providers and healthcare staff are an excellent resource, but nothing can replace the

## I AM RECEIVING RADIATION. IS THERE ANY RISK FOR RADIATION EXPOSURE TO MY FAMILY?

Radiation exposure to others depends on the type of radiation you are receiving. External beam radiation that is delivered on a daily basis offers no risk of radiation emission at home. This would include patients receiving radiation to the lumpectomy site for their breast cancer, to the lung for their lung cancer, or to the rectum for their rectal cancer. Many types of solid tumor cancers, or lymphomas, receive this type of radiation. When radiation is given as an implant or internally and, therefore, the patient is receiving radiation continuously over a period of days to weeks, then there is some risk to family members. A common type of internal radiation is iodine-131, which is used to treat thyroid cancers.

Because radiation therapy is harmful to the chromosomes and cell division, pregnant women and children are at the highest risk for exposure, so it is best to maintain distance until your physician gives you clearance. Bodily fluids are radioactive for a period of time and should be handled with care. Some precautions for family members of patients receiving internal radiation include: sleeping in separate bedrooms, using different bathrooms, washing clothing separately, and using disposable plates/utensils. Your radiation oncologist can give you more specific instructions regarding limiting exposure to family members.

personal experience of someone with your same type of cancer who may be receiving the same treatment, or who may experience the same adverse side effects. Support groups have become a popular resource for many cancer patients. According to the Merriam-Webster dictionary, a support group is a group of people with common experiences and concerns who provide emotional and moral support for one another. With this broad definition, it is no wonder that support groups exist for almost any illness and with almost any purpose. Often, there is no set curriculum for these groups, so each support group is different. They are generally peer led so the discussion is really left up to the group.

If you are looking for a support group, the first place to check would be your local church. I recommend seeking a Christian-based group first because the primary focus of a support group must be on Christ and the encouragement He gives during this journey. The worldly view of cancer is depressing and hopeless; thus, you will find many of the members of a secular group to be depressed and without hope. Sure, it is okay to compare stories and to learn from each other's experiences. That is primarily why people want to attend support groups. But, if the support group does not elevate Christ throughout the cancer journey, then your benefit from the group will likely diminish.

Church groups may not be cancer-specific. They usually encompass many different chronic illnesses. If you desire a cancer-specific group then check with your physician's office to see if they recommend, or facilitate, a particular group. Branches of the American Cancer Society (ACS) are also excellent resources for locating a group, and if the ACS branch is big enough, you will be able to find groups based on cancer type. Finally, with the Internet, you can locate virtually any type of support group online. Remember, with any secular support group, use wisdom and discernment regarding the type of conversation and the general goal of the group.

If finding a support group is difficult, then look for an individual who shares a similar journey. You may find more comfort in a one-on-one relationship than you do in an actual support group. Again, I would recommend a Christian individual whom you trust and can speak to with candor.

## ENCOURAGEMENT FROM THE WORD

*Two are better than one, because they have a good reward for their toil. For if they fall, one will lift up his fellow. But woe to him who is alone when he falls and has not another to lift him up! Again, if two lie together, they keep warm, but how can one keep warm alone? And though a man might prevail against one who is alone, two will withstand him—a threefold cord is not quickly broken.* (Ecclesiastes 4:9-12)

Though not one of their most famous songs, "I Am a Rock" by Simon and Garfunkel represents the difficulty and pain associated with relationships. In their lyrics, they speak of friendship causing pain and crying after loving. Their response to the hurt is to become like a rock, or an island, because "a rock feels no pain, and an island never cries." What an unfortunate conclusion—and one that is not biblically based. Though our sole purpose in this life is to glorify God, God in His kindness and mercy allows us, and encourages us, to have fellowship and communion with others. By way of example, God shares perfect harmony and communion with the other members of the Trinity— God the Son and God the Holy Spirit. Then, in the creation account of Genesis, each and every event was labeled as "good," except for one. "It is not good that the man should be alone; I will make him a helper fit for him" (Genesis 2:18).

While this verse specifically relates to marriage, there are other verses that relate to the body of Christ being the Church. "For the body does not consist of one member but of many" (1 Corinthians 12:14). God designed us to dwell together, serve together, and worship Him together. "And let us consider how to stir up one another to love and good works, not neglecting to meet together, as is the habit of some, but encouraging one another, and all the more as you see the Day drawing near" (Hebrews 10:24-25).

You are fooling yourself if you think the journey through cancer will not affect those around you. They may not have the disease, but family and friends will carry some of the burden of the cancer. Perhaps nothing tests a relationship more than a chronic disease or a season of illness. Cancer can destroy a family, or it can bring one closer together. When it comes to relationships, families, unsaved parents or spouses, grown children, or babies, the dynamics of the family are often molded and shaped by the individual suffering

> Cancer can destroy a family, or it can bring one closer together.

with the disease. You, as the patient, will ultimately decide how the disease, treatment, and surveillance will affect your life and, subsequently, how it will affect your family and friends. Here are a few examples.

Virginia wanted to keep her household in perfect order, but her breast cancer treatment made her very tired. When she ceased to be able to do her daily chores, Virginia's high school daughters pulled together and kept the home the way their mother desired. They learned valuable tools about service and homemaking, while Virginia learned the value of humility. One other example is not quite so pleasant.

Bob's kids were grown and lived some distance away. He had already lost his wife to cancer, so Bob didn't want the children to suffer anymore. Bob decided not to tell his grown children when he was diagnosed with leukemia. He stopped calling them on the phone. He discouraged them from visiting. As a result, their relationship became strained and distant. Bob's kids were shocked when they finally learned the truth and, by this time, Bob had very little time left.

Different families deal with cancer differently. There is no roadmap for how to deal with cancer. Even Christian families often struggle with a trial like cancer because the dynamics of the family can vary based on each individual's personal walk with Christ and on their interactions with those who do not walk with Christ. For example, an unsaved child may be angry and fearful about his mother's diagnosis of terminal cancer. A newly born-again Christian spouse may not fully understand her role in caring for her husband through cancer. Allow me to give you some very simple biblical principles when dealing with your family, friends, and church body. There is no one better to look to than Christ as our example.

First, open and honest communication is essential. Toward the end of Christ's ministry on earth, He began to tell His disciples about His death and resurrection. Christ explained to His disciples "that He must go to Jerusalem and suffer many things from the elders and chief priests and scribes, and be killed, and on the third day be raised" (Matthew 16:21). In Matthew 17:22-23 and Matthew 20:17-19,

Christ repeats the information and again tells His disciples of His death and suffering. Though He often taught the disciples in parable form, when it came to His death and resurrection, He was open and honest with those who were closest to Him.

People, including children, can sense when you are hiding information or pretending like everything is fine. Poor communication brings anxiety and anger to others. Poor communication also sets a bad example for unsaved family members. With those closest to you, it is best to tell them the facts and to put it very simply. They may need it repeated over and over. To a small child, this may mean you simply tell him that you are sick and that you are trusting in God because He knows best. You can ask the child to help you pray to God. An older child or grown adult will require more details. Inviting the individual to a doctor's appointment may allow them an opportunity to ask questions and better understand your cancer. Your church family will also want information, which can be burdensome when so many are asking you the same questions. Devise a way to communicate your information to many people at once—email, for example is a wonderful way to give updates to a large group of people.

Second, continue to serve your family, friends, and local body, even through your trial and suffering. In the hours prior to Christ's arrest, He celebrated the Passover Feast with His disciples. In John

13, Jesus explains to His disciples that they must serve one another. "If I then, your Lord and Teacher, have washed your feet, you also ought to wash one another's feet. For I have given you an example, that you also should do just as I have done to you" (John 13:14-15). We are called to serve one another continually, even through our suffering.

> We are called to serve one another continually, even through our suffering.

After Amy Carmichael fell, causing serious injury to her leg and spine, she was no longer able to serve in the same capacity as she previously did. Amy had founded the Dohnavur Fellowship in South India in 1901 with the purpose of "rescuing babies and children from situations and backgrounds of extreme danger."[43] However, after her accident, she was confined to her bed for most of the rest of her days. Yet her ministry continued. "One kind of service still open to Amy, when pain did not make it impossible, was writing."[44] Though she had a great deal of pain, Amy continued serving Christ. She is the author of 37 books and many letters. In one book, Amy writes about trials, "There is no promise of calm water for any mariner, but our Lord can give the faith that can ride out against any high and proud winds and waves. And He can come to our succor though our sea seemeth all to be on fire."[45] Cancer does not change your ultimate mandate, to do all things to glorify Christ. Cancer does not give you the opportunity to stop serving Christ and, consequently, your family and friends.

Third, embrace the veil of humility that will fall upon you during your cancer journey, and again look to Christ for strength. There can be nothing more humbling than being stripped of clothing and dying on a cross between two criminals. "Have this mind among yourselves, which is yours in Christ Jesus, who, though He was in the form of God, did not count equality with God a thing to be grasped, but made Himself nothing, taking the form of a servant, being born in the likeness of men. And being found in human form, He humbled Himself by becoming obedient to the point of death, even death on a cross" (Philippians 2:5-8).

Recognizing your limitations and asking for help allows others to see you as the human being God created. Unlike Christ, and sometimes seemingly unknown to your family, you do have limitations. Though created in God's image, unfortunately, we have some attributes that God Himself does not have. We have limits. We require sleep. We get sick, we fail because of sin, and the list goes on. Certainly, this is not meant to be discouraging, but rather a refreshing reality. You don't have to play the role of "superhuman." When you acknowledge your frailties and publicly place all your strength on Christ, your life will be a testimony to family and friends.

> When you acknowledge your frailties and publicly place all your strength on Christ, your life will be a testimony to family and friends.

Finally, be prepared for the enemy to strike you, your family, and the church. The cancer journey is not just a battle of the body. It will be a spiritual battle, as well. Job's trial was not simply loss of fortune, death of loved ones, and a painful disease. Satan was present. It was a supernatural battle. The enemy will strike at you in any place, which may include your family. Arm yourself with the tools for battle found in Ephesians 6:13-18. "Therefore take up the whole armor of God, that you may be able to withstand in the evil day, and having done all, to stand firm" (Ephesians 6:13).

The war between God and Satan has already been won by Christ, but you must be prepared for small battles that may cause a ripple in your peaceful waters. A trial is an excellent opportunity for temptations and spiritual weakness to overcome you. Truth, righteousness, and the Gospel have already been given to you. The foundation for your success was established when you believed in Christ. Now you must immerse yourself in the Scriptures, place all your hope in your salvation, and pray without ceasing. Christ will help you conquer each battle with victory. "For because He himself has suffered when tempted, He is able to help those who are being tempted" (Hebrews 2:18).

Are you exhausted by all your new responsibilities? Yes, you are the patient, but you are also the teacher, counselor, servant, and warrior to your family, friends, and church. Your job description has been changed by the cancer. Of course you will need your rest (and many people will be there to remind you), and most definitely, you will need to eat well (and many people will come as close as possible to opening your mouth and shoving the food in), but these new tasks will require the spiritual rest and food that only Christ can provide. Embrace this new role that the Lord has laid before you. As David Powlison expands on John Piper's "Don't Waste Your Cancer," he advises, "Paradoxically, moving out into relationships when you are hurting and weak will actually strengthen others…Your need gives others an opportunity to love. And since love is always God's highest purpose in you, too, you will learn His finest and most joyous lessons as you find small ways to express concern for others even when you are most weak."[46]

# CHAPTER TEN

# FINDING ETERNITY

Jennifer was diagnosed with ovarian cancer about five years ago. Despite several doses of chemotherapy, her cancer continued to grow. She would receive treatment, and then have a few months of "normal" living before the tumor marker would start to rise. Gradually, however, the months turned into a few weeks and, finally, she began to progress while receiving the chemotherapy. It was no longer working. She was constantly nauseated and vomited about three times per day. She had a lot of abdominal pain from the cancer that had implanted in the wall of her abdomen. She was tired—tired of being sick, tired of fighting, and simply tired of being tired.

On a particular day in September, I had the pleasure of speaking with her regarding her chemotherapy. She was tearful about her future. Part of her wanted to stop treatment, but the other part of her knew stopping the treatment meant speeding up her death. She had family in Arizona she wanted to see and had meant to go, but she just never got around to it. Her questions were the typical questions I hear at this stage of life: How much time do I have left? What is the normal process of dying? Will I be in pain? Before we attempt to answer these questions, let me give you a word of caution: If your cancer is curable then rejoice in your cure. Your end may not be from cancer, but we will all die one day unless the Lord returns. He will call you home at His perfect time.

THE FAST TRACK

We've come to the chapter that probably no one wants to read, but everyone is curious about. It is the one experience that no one can help you through or give you advice about. Death is the one road all of us will travel alone. You have heard the saying, "Death is just a part of life." That saying may be true, but when God created Adam and Eve to live and dwell with Him in paradise, there was no such thing as death. It wasn't until sin entered the world that death entered the world. Yes, we are all going to die because sin has entered the world, and the wages of sin is death (Romans 6:23). But some of us have now moved to the "fast-track" of death. "For everything there is a season, and a time for every matter under heaven: a time to be born, and a time to die" (Ecclesiastes 3:1-2). If this is your season to die, then allow this chapter to be a guide to the physical aspects of death and a reminder of the eternal life that awaits those who believe in Jesus Christ.

What, specifically, occurs to our physical bodies when we die? In the medical world, a patient is considered dead when the heart muscle ceases to contract and the brain ceases to send and receive information from the body. Contraction of the heart muscle is vital to living because that contraction delivers blood to all parts of the body. Red blood cells in the blood carry oxygen, and all cells require oxygen to perform the major chemical reactions for cellular life. If cells do not receive oxy-

## SHOULD I HAVE A FEEDING TUBE PLACED?

This question is often asked by family members who are struggling to see their loved ones dying. I am often told, "I understand he is going to die, but I don't want him to starve to death in the process." It is very challenging and frustrating to watch someone slowly fade away, but unfortunately it is also part of the natural progression of terminal cancer. When thinking of end of life care, feeding tubes are not typically recommended. At this stage, patients are often not hungry and are, therefore, not "starving." Increasing food, or utilizing a feeding tube, can actually make the patient more uncomfortable or cause an increase in nausea. In cancer care, feeding tubes are often used for preserving weight and nutrition during active treatment such as gastric (stomach) cancers, esophageal cancers, or head/neck cancers.

gen, they will try to make it themselves, but they will never be able to produce enough oxygen to keep up the necessary demands of the body. Perhaps the most important organ requiring oxygen is the brain. If the brain does not receive oxygen, then it will become damaged and, ultimately, stop working. The brain controls everything in the body, including the most basic and subconscious ability of breathing.

Oxygen is not the only major requirement for life. Glucose is also required for the body to function properly (see Chapter 8). In a cancer patient that is no longer receiving treatment, or who is receiving treatment that is no longer working, the cancer begins to take over the body. Cancer requires more and more of the nutrients in the body for survival, thus starving the body and depriving it from those essential nutrients. Glucose is the most basic energy source for the body. If the cancer cells are stealing all the glucose, then the body will begin to break down protein and fat to feed itself. As the body begins to starve, it will weaken and perform only the necessary activities. The brain will require glucose to continue functioning and will, therefore, take the highest priority. Normal activities become more difficult, and the patient begins to limit their energy expenditure to the most basic needs, resorting to lying down for much of their day. Finally, the patient begins to sleep more and drift into a comatose state until, at last, their breathing becomes erratic and their heart stops.

There are some ways to alter, or delay, this normal process of dying. Modern medicine has developed some amazing procedures, drugs, and technology to maintain life. Cardiopulmonary

Resuscitation (CPR), ventilation machines, and medications like epinephrine are very good tools and definitely have a place in medicine. I will not begin to expand on the controversy that lies with the use of all of these tools, but all of us are going to die one day, whether we use these tools or not. No tool or drug has the power to change that fact or supersede the ultimate, sovereign hand of God. What I do want to present to you are the options that are available.

By law, medical doctors are required to use all means necessary to save a life. CPR is the use of pressure to the chest wall to force the heart to circulate the blood, thus circulating oxygen, when it is no longer beating. CPR works, but not without consequences. A cancer patient that has disease in the bones will be more susceptible to rib fractures and a collapsed lung when CPR is performed. A defibrillator machine utilizes an electrical shock to allow the heart to start beating again. The heart works by sending an electrical signal throughout the muscle to contract, and that contraction pushes the blood through the body. By shocking the heart, you are allowing it to "reset" itself in hopes that the electrical current will resume correctly.

Ventilation machines are used when an individual can no longer provide enough oxygen to support their body. This can be in cases where damage has occurred to the brain and the brain no longer tells the body when to take a breath or when the lungs are no longer capable of taking in an adequate breath. Ventilation machines, while a great "life-saving" tool, also have adverse effects associated with them. Patients are more susceptible to infection and, the longer you stay on a ventilation machine, the more difficult it becomes for you to be weaned off the machine. Finally, there are many medications that can be use to aid the body—some that increase the heart rate, some that slow the heart rate, some that raise blood pressure, and some that lower blood pressure. The vast array of medications available is truly wonderful and can save lives, but there is a side effect associated with every medication.

LEGAL DOCUMENTS

With all of these technological and pharmaceutical advances, decision making is important for end of life care. An advance directive is a legal document that allows you to declare what type of treatment you wish to have should you become incapable of making a decision. This part of the advance directive is called a living will. The second part of an advance directive is called a power of attorney, and in this section you can designate someone to make medical decisions for you should you become incapable. The form and documentation can vary from state to state, so it is important to become familiar with your state's requirements. Most forms will present several scenarios and will ask how you want your health care to be dealt with in these certain scenarios. Once you have completed the form, it will likely need to be notarized and witnessed.

A DNR is another document used in end of life care. DNR stands for "Do Not Resuscitate," and it is the decision to tell medical providers not to perform any lifesaving measures. In other words, no CPR, defibrillation, ventilation, or medications are to be used for the purpose of saving a life. This document is primarily used in a hospital setting, and the rules vary as to how EMS/EMT personnel handle DNRs. Most emergency medical services require a separate form and will perform CPR in the field if this form is not presented to them upon arrival. This makes sense, as the purpose of emergency medical services is to do everything possible to save a life. If there are some services you would like performed, then you can be more specific in your advance directive. For example, some patients chose a "chemical code only," which means medications can be given to try and restart the heart, but CPR and defibrillation will not be utilized.

Certainly, documenting your end-of-life decisions are important, but even more important is verbalizing your wishes to family and friends. Sam did not communicate his wishes to his three adult children. When his breathing became so poor from the lung cancer and emphysema, he was placed on a ventilator machine in an emergency situation. The family was torn with all the decisions that needed to be made regarding his care. They so desperately wanted to know what their father's wishes were, but it was too late to ask him. Preparing in advance, and expressing your wishes to family and friends, will ease both your anxiety about the dying process and the burden placed upon family and friends when that time comes.

## HOSPICE VERSUS PALLIATIVE CARE

Besides all the legal decisions and paperwork that occur toward the end of life, there are several options for end-of-life care. Hospice is probably the most well-known model for end-of-life care. It is primarily used to provide pain control and comfort measures to dying people. By definition, hospice care is for patients who have a terminal illness with only six months left to live. By terminal illness, this could be cancer, AIDS, stroke or heart disease. Most health insurance companies have a special benefit for hospice care, and Medicare uses part A for hospice benefits. If your health insurance does not cover hospice, or you do not have any insurance, there are some hospice agencies that provide care based on the donations they receive. Hospice can be begun through the inpatient or hospital setting, or it can be done in the comfort of your own home. Typically, a patient is referred to a hospice agency by a physician like your oncologist, but you can also seek hospice agencies without a referral.

Most hospice agencies have a medical director to oversee patient care. This can be concerning for some patients, as they feel their oncologist will no longer be in charge of their care. Our practice generally assures our patients that we are still available and will see them at any time, but the idea of hospice is to keep the patient at home so that they don't have to come out for doctor's appointments. Once you enter hospice care, then you are no longer able to receive treatment in the curative/control setting. Patients often assume that

## WILL I BE IN PAIN WHEN I'M DYING?

It is important to remember that not all cancer patients experience pain, but some patients do experience tremendous pain. Pain is usually present in the area where the cancer is present— bone pain, if it is in the bones or abdominal pain if it is present in the abdomen. Pain control is very important in end-of-life care, and it can be achieved. There are several classes of medications for pain control, and all relieve pain in a different way. Most physicians who are experienced in pain management will use a variety of medications for pain control. The class of medications most commonly used for pain control is the narcotic family. This class has received a bad reputation, but it probably provides the best pain relief. Pain control is important for comfort and rest. Pain that is not well-controlled causes anxiety, increased blood pressure, and other stressors on the body.

When attempting to control pain, it is best to stop it before it peaks. Once pain has gotten severe, it will require more medication to bring it under control. Long-acting narcotics are typically used to keep the pain at a low level throughout the day. Should the pain not be adequately controlled, then breakthrough medications can be used periodically. As I have mentioned several times before, all medications have side effects. The narcotic class of medication causes drowsiness and constipation. I typically tell people to take something for constipation (see Chapter 4 on constipation) each time they take pain medication. Developing a "bowel" regimen to manage constipation is extremely important. In a few patients, narcotics can cause nausea and vomiting.

you can no longer receive any type of treatment once utilizing hospice services; however, treatment can be given for palliation— to assist with symptom control such as radiation treatment for pain.

Hospice agencies are able to provide medications for pain and other symptoms. This means you typically do not have to leave your home and go to the pharmacy to pick up prescriptions. If hospice care seems a bit too much for you right now, then palliative care might be an option. There is very little difference between palliative care and hospice, but, generally, palliative care does allow you to continue receiving treatment in the curative/control setting.

## ENCOURAGEMENT FROM THE WORD

*For we know that if the tent that is our earthly home is destroyed, we have a building from God, a house not made with hands, eternal in the heavens. For in this tent we groan, longing to put on our heavenly dwelling, if indeed by putting it on we may not be found naked. For while we are still in this tent, we groan, being burdened—not that we would be unclothed, but that we would be further clothed, so that what is mortal may be swallowed up by life. He who has prepared us for this very thing is God, who has given us the Spirit as a guarantee. So we are always of good courage. We know that while we are at home in the body we are away from the Lord, for we walk by faith, not by sight. Yes, we are of good courage, and we would rather be away from the body and at home with the Lord. (2 Corinthians 5:1-8)*

Dr. C.W. Smith, in his commencement address to the 2002 graduating class of The Master's College, called cancer "the kind killer." He described death by cancer as kind because "it gives us warning of impending death."[47] As opposed to a sudden/accidental death, cancer gives us a period of time to get our affairs in order, prepare our family and friends for our departure, examine our faith, and to set aside all meaningless works and place our entire focus on worshipping and loving our God.

Yes, cancer may be the "kind" killer, but that does not make it easy. In my line of work, I have seen many deaths. I have seen peaceful deaths, and I've seen deaths that are full of anxiety and fear. I have seen people who welcome death like a cozy blanket, for they know their suffering will cease, and they will dwell with their Savior. Then there are those that fight death as though they are caught in a bed of quicksand. Christian, the pilgrim from John Bunyan's *The Pilgrim's Progress*, found himself struggling through the River of Death when trying to cross to the Celestial City, while Hopeful, his good friend and companion, found ground to stand upon when crossing.[48] While there is a correlation between the Christian walk and the ease with which one dies, there are many variables to this measurement that only God can ascertain. Our walk with Christ is one of perfecting sanctification, and we are all at different stages at different times. Learning to die is just another trial to endure and the final piece in perfecting your relationship with Christ.

If you are finding deep waters as you swim through the River of Death, then I pray this chapter will help you find firm footing, for Heaven is the most joyful topic in this entire book. Heaven—a word that describes paradise, perfect harmony, and

> Learning to die is just another trial to endure and the final piece in perfecting your relationship with Christ.

loss of pain for those who believe in Christ. If you have put your faith in Christ, and if He is Lord over your earthly life, then paradise awaits you. But Heaven is more than paradise. For the believer, it is a re-uniting with Christ and a restoration of our sinful souls to a perfect soul. We will be holy and righteous.

We have already learned that the origin of death is sin. Death entered this world when Adam and Eve sinned in the garden. "By the sweat of your face you shall eat bread, till you return to the ground, for out of it you were taken; for you are dust, and to dust you shall return" (Genesis 3:19). Now death is part of all our lives because of the original sin in the garden. In fact, very few biblical men have escaped the clutches of death. Unfortunately, we are not all Elijahs who have the privilege of going to Heaven by a whirlwind (2 Kings 2:11). Christians and non-Christians alike will experience illness, aging, and death of the physical body. Though death is part of the punishment for sin, as believers in Christ, death is not our punishment. It is simply the consequence of living in a sinful world. Christians suffer no punishment from God because God only sees the imputed righteousness of Christ when He looks upon us.

Yet death is associated with pain and suffering—even for Christians. Cancer, for example, can be a very painful disease in the end—not just physically, but also emotionally and spiritually. It seems challenging to look upon death with anticipation and eagerness when we know the process may be difficult. Much like any of our trials through this life, and what we have discussed throughout this book, death is the last opportunity for Christ to complete His work in you. Job explains God's purpose in his many trials, "...when He has tried me, I shall come out as gold" (Job 23:10).

Death is the final completion of our sanctification, and it is our final encounter with sin. Through Christ we are able to conquer that last battle and, in the end, we will be refined by the fire into pure gold. We will be united with Christ and made perfect. Death *is* victory for the believer. Once we cross over from our earthly dwelling to our heavenly dwelling, then we will be victorious over sin. "When the perishable puts on the imperishable, and the mortal puts on immortality, then

> Death *is* victory for the believer.

shall come to pass the saying that is written: 'Death is swallowed up in victory. O death, where is your victory? O death, where is your sting?' The sting of death is sin, and the power of sin is the law. But thanks be to God, who gives us the victory through our Lord Jesus Christ" (1 Corinthians 15:54-57).

Question #1 of "The Heidelberg Catechism" asks, "What is your only comfort in life and in death? That I am not my own, but belong with body and soul, both in life and in death, to my faithful Saviour Jesus Christ. He has fully paid for all my sins with His precious blood, and has set me free from all the power of the devil. He also preserves me in such a way that without the will of my heavenly Father not a hair can fall from my head; indeed, all things must work together for my salvation. Therefore, by His Holy Spirit He also assures me of eternal life and makes me heartily willing and ready from now on to live for Him."[49] Truly, this is a comforting thought. We belong to Christ. He governs every aspect of our lives, and nothing will disrupt our lives unless it is willed by the Father. We will not depart from this earth until our Heavenly Father is ready to take us home. Our departure to be with Christ will occur at the perfect time.

When our departure does occur, we will be immediately united with Christ. There is no special place for our soul to reside and wait while we carry out our sin sentence. There is no slumber in the cold ground while we wait for Christ to return. 2 Corinthians 5:6-8 gives the Christian only two choices: We are either "at home in the body," meaning alive on earth, or "at home with the Lord." When Jesus was hanging on the cross, suffering the physical death of man, He turned to the criminal that believed and said, "Truly, I say to you, *today* you will be with Me in Paradise" (Luke 23:43, emphasis added). Christ did not say, "you will be with Me after you've had a long sleep in the ground when I decide to come back in a few thousand years." No, Christ gave the criminal the gift of instantaneous union. Christ gives us the gift of instantaneous union as well. Once we have breathed our last breath and our hearts have ceased to beat, we will be with Him in paradise.

> Once we have breathed our last breath and our hearts have ceased to beat, we will be with Him in paradise.

The story does not end there. It just gets better. Although we have departed our earthly bodies and are united with Christ, we are still "naked" (2 Corinthians 5:3). Our souls are with Christ and are perfected, but our physical bodies are buried. Sanctification was our earthly journey to know Christ better, be more like Him, and serve Him perfectly. Glorification will be the absolute restoration of our whole bodies and the completion of our redemption. Our glorification will not be complete until Christ returns and raises our physical bodies from the grave. Our physical bodies will not be old and ugly. They will be "imperishable" (1 Corinthians 15:42).

The final chapter of this eternal life, Heaven as it is called in the Bible, will be a life of full enjoyment and communion with God. After the final judgment, God will create a new dwelling for His people. "Then I saw a new heaven and a new earth, for the first heaven and the first earth had passed away, and the sea was no more" (Revelation 21:1). Revelation 21 and 22 tells us about "The New Jerusalem." The walls are built high, with the foundations of each wall being adorned with jewels like sapphires, emeralds, amethysts, and jasper. Between the walls are gates that are made of single pearls. Once inside the city, the streets are laid with pure gold. There is a garden—perhaps like the Garden of Eden—where there are trees that yield twelve kinds of fruit and a beautiful crystal river flowing through the middle of the street. Revelation 21:23 says, "the city has no need of sun or moon to shine on it, for the glory of God gives it light, and its lamp is the Lamb." There will be no night or darkness in this city.

Though we may marvel and dream at the thought of our new home, we must not lose sight of our new career. Our heavenly vocation will be devoted to worshipping the Lord. We will do this without needing a vacation, without becoming weary from a hard day's work, and without a year-end bonus. Contrary to our worship in this life, which is based on faith, our worship with God will be easy and without hindrance. We will dwell with God and see Him face to face (Revelation 22:4). "And I heard a loud voice from the throne saying, "'Behold, the dwelling place of God is with man. He will dwell with them, and they will be His people, and God Himself will be with them as their God. He will wipe away every tear from their eyes, and death shall be no more, neither shall there be mourning, nor crying, nor pain anymore, for the former things have passed away'" (Revelation 21:3-4).

If you have reached this final chapter, then you have not yet reached the Celestial City. Perhaps you are on the verge of entering the River of Death, or perhaps you are already swimming in it. Have no fear of this final journey. Instead, meditate on the words of Charles Spurgeon, "Within a very little time thou shalt be rid of all thy trials and thy troubles. Thine eyes now suffused with tears shall weep no longer. Thou shalt gaze in ineffable rapture upon the splendour of Him who sits upon the throne. Nay, more, upon His throne shalt thou sit. The triumph of His glory shall be shared by thee; His crown, His joy, His paradise, these shall be thine, and thou shalt be co-heir with Him who is the heir of all things."[50] May we all find death to be filled with peace, joy, and hope.

# APPENDIX A

# GOSPEL MESSAGE TO UNBELIEVERS

There can be no mistake that you have happened upon this book. Perhaps you were drawn in by the title or are looking for any help you can find through this cancer journey. Perhaps a Christian family member or friend gave you a copy in hopes that you might find comfort from Christ. Whatever the reason, I encourage you to keep reading because there is more at stake here than just your physical health. No doubt, cancer is a terrifying disease, and you are looking for hope, but the disease of sin is a far greater calamity and one that will claim your soul for eternity if you do not put your faith in Jesus Christ. How do you begin to put your faith in Christ and believe in Him? First, you must recognize your need for a relationship with Christ. You must recognize your need for the Savior.

When God created man and woman, He did so in His own image. Their creation was pleasing to Him and He felt it was "very good" (Genesis 1:31). Then sin entered the world through Satan's temptation of Eve in the Garden of Eden. From that point on, humans were separated from God—separated because God is sinless, hates all sin, and will punish all those guilty of sin. Sin causes eternal death, and because of the original sin in the garden, we are all now guilty of sin. The separation is so great that no human can bridge the gap or re-gain access to God. Only God can amend the separation and reconcile the relationship. Thus, in His mercy and because He loves His creation, God made plans for a redeemer. From the very beginning, God planned for Jesus Christ, His Son, to be the sacrifice necessary to save His people from their sin (Genesis 3:15). "For there is one God, and there is one mediator between God and men, the man Christ Jesus, who gave Himself as a ransom for all" (1 Timothy 2:5-6).

Christ came to this earth to live the perfect life and to be the perfect sacrifice. 1 Peter 2:24 says, "He Himself bore our sins in His body on the tree, that we might die to sin and live to righteousness. By His wounds you have been healed." Christ's purpose in coming to earth as the perfect man—to provide the necessary payment for our sin—was fulfilled when He died on the cross at Calvary. His death was the ultimate sacrifice necessary to remove the barrier between

God and humans. The only access we have to God is through Jesus Christ. In John 14:6, Jesus tells His disciples, "I am the way, and the truth, and the life. No one comes to the Father except through Me." We must place our faith and trust in Christ to gain access and be in relationship with our Heavenly Father. Doing good deeds, living a moral life, working hard, or giving money to charity, will not purchase you a relationship with God. His mercy and grace are given freely to those who believe in Christ.

To receive God's mercy and be reconciled to Him, you must accept Christ and ask Him to be the ruler of your heart and life. "But to all who did receive Him, who believed in His name, He gave the right to become children of God, who were born, not of blood nor of the will of the flesh nor of the will of man, but of God (John 1:12-13)." Becoming a believer and a child of God will not likely cure your cancer, but it will give you a future of hope. Eternal death is the end result for all non-believers regardless of any physical illness, but eternal life is guaranteed to all who accept Christ. Christ desires for each one of us to call upon Him and accept Him as Savior and Ruler over our lives.

Perhaps you think surrendering your life to Christ will not be helpful because He does not know what you are going through or how you are feeling. You may think that God is distant and not interested in you. You are mistaken! Christ came to this Earth to experience life as a man, and to ultimately die that you may live. You can always find comfort in a Savior who experienced more difficult challenges than you could ever think or imagine, and that includes your fight with cancer. "Blessed be the God and Father of our Lord Jesus Christ, the Father of mercies and God of all comfort, who comforts us in *all* our affliction." (2 Corinthians 1:3-4, emphasis added).

Finally, friend, I want to share with you may favorite verse: "Come to Me, all who labor and are heavy laden, and I will give you rest. Take My yoke upon you, and learn from Me, for I am gentle and lowly in heart, and you will find rest for your souls" (Matthew 11:28-29). Christ not only offers comfort and mercy, but He is a safe haven as well—a place where we can run when we are weary and when our troubles and burdens become too great to carry.

My prayer for you, whether you believe in the saving grace of Christ or whether you are struggling to give your life over to Him, is that you will unload all of your burdens—the burden of sin, the burden of living in a sinful world, and the burden of your cancer—to the only One that can carry them. When your journey with cancer is finished, I pray that your Heavenly Father will reward you for finishing the race, and that you can say, with Paul, "I have fought the good fight, I have finished the race, I have kept the faith (2 Timothy 4:7)."

# RISK OF NAUSEA AND VOMITING ASSOCIATED WITH CHEMOTHERAPY

## High

Carmustine (high doses)
Cisplatin (high doses)
Cyclophosphamide (high doses)
Dacarbazine (high doses)
Doxorubicin (high doses)
Epirubicin (high doses)
Ifosfamide (high doses)
Mechlorethamine
Streptozocin

## Moderate

Aldesleukin (high doses)
Amifostine
Arsenic trioxide
Azacitidine
Bendamustine
Busulfan
Carboplatin

Carmustine
Clofarabine
Cyclophosphamide
Cytarabine
Dactinomycin
Daunorubicin
Doxorubicin
Epirubicin
Idarubicin
Ifosfamide
Interferon alfa (high doses)
Irinotecan
Melphalan
Methotrexate (high doses)
Oxaliplatin
Temozolomide

| Low | Minimal |
|---|---|
| Amifostine (low doses) | Alemtuzumab |
| Aldesleukin (low doses) | Asparaginase |
| Brentuximab vedotin | Bevacizumab |
| Cabazitaxel | Bleomycin |
| Carfilzomib | Bortezomib |
| Cytarabine (low dose) | Capecitabine |
| Docetaxel | Cetuximab |
| Doxorubicin liposomal | Cladribine |
| Eribulin | Cytarabine (low doses) |
| Etoposide | Decitabine |
| 5-FU | Denileukin diftitox |
| Floxuridine | Dexrazoxane |
| Gemcitabine | Fludarabine |
| Interferon alpha | Interferon alpha (low doses) |
| Ixabepilone | Ipilimumab |
| Methotrexate | Methotrexate (low doses) |
| Mitomycin | Nelarabine |
| Mitoxantrone | Ofatumumab |
| Paclitaxel | Panitumumab |
| Paclitaxel albumin | Pegaspargase |
| Pemetrexed | Peginterferon |
| Pentostatin | Pertuzumab |
| Pralatrexate | Rituximab |
| Romidepsin | Temsirolimus |
| Thiotepa | Trastuzumab |
| Topotecan | Valrubicin |
| Cytarabine | Vinblastine |
| Temozolomide | Vincristine |
| | Vincristine liposomal |
| | Vinorelbine |

# APPENDIX C

# CANCER LOG BOOK

Name: _____

Date of Birth: _____

Address: _____

Provider Information

| Specialty | Name | Phone |
|---|---|---|
| Primary Care MD | | |
| Surgeon | | |
| Oncologist | | |
| Radiation Oncologist | | |
| | | |
| | | |

## Personal Health Information

Past history: _____

Past surgeries: _____

Current medications: _____

_____

_____

Allergies: _____

Family history: _____

_____

_____

## Cancer History

Age at diagnosis: _____

Cancer type/location: _____

Stage at diagnosis: _____

Pathological features: _____

## Treatment Summary

**Surgery:**

Date of surgery: _____

Location of surgery: _____

Type of operation: _____

Complications: _____

Date of surgery: _____

Location of surgery: _____

Type of operation: _____

Complications: _____


Date of surgery: _____

Location of surgery: _____

Type of operation: _____

Complications: _____

## Radiation:

Dates of radiation: _____

Location of radiation: _____

Amount of radiation: _____

Complications: _____


Dates of radiation: _____

Location of radiation: _____

Amount of radiation: _____

Complications: _____

## Chemotherapy/Biotherapy/Hormone therapy:

| Date | Cycle | Drug | Complications |
|------|-------|------|---------------|
|      |       |      |               |
|      |       |      |               |
|      |       |      |               |
|      |       |      |               |
|      |       |      |               |

| Date | Cycle | Drug | Complications |
|------|-------|------|---------------|
|      |       |      |               |
|      |       |      |               |
|      |       |      |               |
|      |       |      |               |
|      |       |      |               |

| Date | Cycle | Drug | Complications |
|------|-------|------|---------------|
|      |       |      |               |
|      |       |      |               |
|      |       |      |               |
|      |       |      |               |
|      |       |      |               |

## Other:

_____

_____

_____

_____

## Post-treatment complications:

1._____

2._____

3._____

4._____

5._____

<u>Surveillance</u>

## Oncologist visit:

| Date/Interval | Discussion |
|---------------|------------|
|               |            |
|               |            |
|               |            |
|               |            |
|               |            |
|               |            |

| Date/Interval | Discussion |
|---|---|
|  |  |
|  |  |
|  |  |
|  |  |
|  |  |
|  |  |

| Date/Interval | Discussion |
|---|---|
|  |  |
|  |  |
|  |  |
|  |  |
|  |  |
|  |  |

Radiation oncologist visit:

| Date/Interval | Discussion |
|---|---|
|  |  |
|  |  |
|  |  |
|  |  |
|  |  |

| | |
|---|---|
| | |
| | |

| Date/Interval | Discussion |
|---|---|
| | |
| | |
| | |
| | |
| | |
| | |

Lab studies:

| Test | Date Drawn | Result |
|---|---|---|
| | | |
| | | |
| | | |
| | | |
| | | |
| | | |

| Test | Date Drawn | Result |
|---|---|---|
| | | |
| | | |

| | | |
|---|---|---|
| | | |
| | | |
| | | |
| | | |

## Imaging studies:

| Name of Study | Date | Result |
|---|---|---|
| | | |
| | | |
| | | |
| | | |
| | | |
| | | |

| Name of Study | Date | Result |
|---|---|---|
| | | |
| | | |
| | | |
| | | |
| | | |
| | | |

# GLOSSARY OF MEDICAL TERMS

**Advanced directive** - a legal document that allows you to declare what type of treatment you wish to have should you become incapable of making a decision

**Alopecia** – hair loss

**Alternative medicine** – the use of alternative treatments to replace conventional medical care

**Amino acid** – the building blocks of proteins

**Anemia** – low red blood cells

**Apoptosis** – cell death

**Attending physician** – the physician who is primarily in charge of you during your hospital stay

**BRCA** – a hereditary mutation known to increase the risk of breast and ovarian cancer

**Cancer** - the repeated replication or duplication of a cell that has a mistake in its information system (DNA)

**Cell** – the basic structural unit of the human body

**Chemotherapy** - the use of chemicals to destroy cancer cells

**Chemotherapy cycles** – a schedule of how chemotherapy is given

**Chills** – or rigors; the exaggerated shivering of the body

**Chromosome** – tightly coiled DNA; the human body has 23 pairs of chromosomes

**Clinical trial** – a research study consisting of human subjects with the purpose of determining the safety and efficacy of new therapies

**Complementary medicine** – when an alternative treatment is used in conjunction with conventional medical care

**Constipation** – a decrease in the number of stools in a given period of time or the hardening of stool

**Consulting physician** – a specialist who is asked to address a specific concern during your hospital stay

**CPR** – cardiopulmonary resuscitation, a technique using artificial respiration and external chest compressions to provide oxygenated blood flow to the brain and heart

**Debulking** – a surgical procedure to remove as much of the cancer as possible; primarily seen in ovarian cancer

**Diarrhea** – an increase in the frequency of stools or a change in the consistency of the stool to soft or watery

**DNA** - deoxyribonucleic acid, the information system of our body

**DNR** – do not resuscitate; a legal document to tell medical providers not to perform any lifesaving measures

**Fatigue** – the loss of energy or the inability to do regular activities due to excessive tiredness

**Fatty acid** – the building blocks of a lipid molecule

**Fever** – temperature greater than 100.5 F

**Gene** – a short segment of DNA that provides the necessary information for production of necessary components in the cell

**Gluconeogenesis** – the formation of glucose from non-carbohydrate sources, primarily done in the liver

**Gray (Gy)** – a unit of measurement for the energy absorbed from ionizing radiation

**Hereditary cancer** – cancer caused by an inherited mutation; suspected in patients with a significant family history or development of cancer at a young age

**HIPPA** – the protection of health information as mandated by the Federal government

**Hospice** – a model for end-of-life care with the philosophy of dying with comfort and dignity

**Lymphatic system** – part of the circulatory system that aids the immune system in fighting infections

**Megakaryocyte** – the particular cell generated in the bone marrow that will form the platelets

**Mucositis** – damage to the tissues of the mouth resulting in the formation of sores or ulcers

**Mutation** – a change in genetic material

**Nadir** – the period of time after chemotherapy when the blood cells are at their lowest level

**Nausea** – unpleasant "wavelike" experience or urge to vomit, associated with sweating, paleness, and weakness

**Neuropathy** – damage to the nerve cells causing numbness or tingling

**Neutropenia** – low neutrophils (a specific white blood cell necessary for fighting infection)

**Neutropenic fever** – the combination of low neutrophils and a fever; this is considered an emergency

**Oncology** – the study of cancer

**Palliative care** – interventions to help with comfort; usually a step before hospice care

**Performance status** – a subjective measurement based on how much a patient is capable of doing without the assistance of another individual

**Radiation** – the use of ionizing radioactive particles to kill, or shrink, cancer cells

**Replication** – the duplication of a strand of DNA

**Sievert** – a unit of measurement of ionizing radiation, used when monitoring the biological danger of radiation

**Surveillance** – close observation

**Targeted agents** – chemical agents not classified as chemotherapy because they act on specific characteristics of the cancer cell

**Thrombocytopenia** – low platelets

**Vomiting** – act of expelling contents from the stomach and small bowel through the mouth

# REFERENCES

1. Myriad Genetic Laboratories, Inc., http://www.myriadtests.com.
2. *Oncogenes, Tumor Suppressor Genes, and Cancer.* The American Cancer Society, http://www.cancer.org/Cancer/CancerCauses/GeneticsandCancer/On cogenesandTumorSuppressorGenes/oncogenes-tumor-suppressor-genes-and-cancer-what-are-mutations.
3. Wagner, J.C., C.A. Sleggs, and P. Marchand, "Diffuse pleural mesothelioma and asbestos exposure in the North Western Cape Province." *Br J Ind Med*, 1960. 17: p. 260.
4. Steele, D.N. and C.C. Thomas, *The five points of Calvinism: defined, defended, documented.* International library of philosophy and theology: Biblical and theological studies. Philadelphia: Presbyterian and Reformed Pub. Co., 1963.
5. Pink, A.W., *The sovereignty of God.* Swengel, Pennsylvania: Bible Truth Depot, 1959.
6. Grudem, W.A., *Systematic theology: an introduction to biblical doctrine.* Grand Rapids, Mich.: Zondervan Pub. House, 1994.
7. Sproul, R.C., *Chosen by God.* Wheaton, Ill.: Tyndale House Publishers, 1986.
8. *Surveillance Epidemiology and End Results (SEER).* National Cancer Institute, http://seer.cancer.gov/statistics/index.html.
9. Perez, C.A., *Principles and practice of radiation oncology.* 4th ed. Philadelphia: Lippincott Williams & Wilkins, 2004.
10. Carson, D.A., *A call to spiritual reformation : priorities from Paul and his prayers.* Grand Rapids, Mich.: Baker Book House, 1992.

11. Bunyan, J., *Prayer*. Puritan paperbacks. London, England: Banner of Truth Trust, 1965.

12. Bounds, E.M., *The complete works of E.M. Bounds on prayer*. Grand Rapids, Mich.: Baker Book House, 1990. p. 275-279.

13. Sproul, R.C. and K.A. Mathison, *The Reformation study Bible: English Standard version, containing the Old and New Testaments*. Orlando, Fla.: Ligonier Ministries, 2005. p. 29.

14. Spurgeon, C.H. *Jehovah-Jireh*, 1884. https://play.google.com/books/reader?id=HY9mm1SWAKQC&printsec=frontcover&output=reader&authuser=0&hl=en&pg=GBS.PA315

15. Newton, J., W. Cowper, and Pre-1801 Imprint Collection (Library of Congress), *Olney hymns: in three books*. Vol. 1. London, England: Printed and sold by W. Oliver, 1779. Hymn 7.

16. *National Digestive Diseases Information Clearinghouse*. National Institutes of Health 2007; 07-2754, http://digestive.niddk.nih.gov/ddiseases/pubs/constipation.

17. *What are the Risks of a Blood Transfusion?* National Heart Lung and Blood Institute 2012, http://www.nhlbi.nih.gov/health/health-topics/topics/bt/risks.html.

18. Spurgeon, C.H., *The Treasury of David*. Peabody, Massachusetts: Hendrickson Publishers, 1988.

19. Sproul, R.C., *Surprised by suffering: the role of pain and death in the Christian life*. Lake Mary, Fla.: Reformation Trust Pub, 2009.

20. National Comprehensive Cancer Network, http://www.nccn.org/professionals/physician_gls/f_guidelines.asp.

21. *Radiation Dose Chart*. http://xkcd.com/radiation/.

22. *X-ray Risk*. http://www.xrayrisk.com/index.php.

23. Fischbach, F.T. and M.B. Dunning, *A manual of laboratory and diagnostic tests*. 7th ed. Philadelphia: Williams & Wilkins, 2004.

24. *Tumor Markers*. American Cancer Society, http://www.cancer.org/Treatment/UnderstandingYourDiagnosis/ExamsandTestDescriptions/TumorMarkers/tumor-markers-specific-markers.

25. MacArthur, J. *The Sufficiency of God's Grace*, 1990. http://www.gty.org/resources/sermons/80-72/the-sufficiency-of-gods-grace.

26. Galli, M. and T. Olsen, *131 Christians everyone should know*. Holman Reference. Nashville, Tenn.: Broadman & Holman, 2000.

27. *What We Do.* U.S. Food and Drug Administration, http://www.fda.gov/aboutfda/whatwedo/default.htm

28. *Illustrative Pharmaceutical Lifecycle.* The Pharmaceutical Research and Manufacturers of America (PhRMA), http://www.phrma.org/sites/default/files/2104/phrma_pharmalifecycle_20120222.pdf

29. Pray, L., *Gleevec: the Breakthrough in Cancer Treatment.* Nature Education, 2008.

30. *National Center for Complementary and Alternative Medicine.* National Institues of Health, http://nccam.nih.gov/.

31. Cabanillas, F., "Vitamin C and cancer: what can we conclude--1,609 patients and 33 years later?" *P R Health Sci J*, 2010. 29(3).

32. Piper, J., *Don't waste your life.* Wheaton, Ill.: Crossway Books, 2003.

33. Ryle, J.C., *Holiness: its nature, hindrances, difficulties, and roots.* Moody Classics. Chicago: Moody Publishers, 2010.

34. Warburg, O., "On the origin of cancer cells." *Science,* 1956. 123(3191): p. 309.

35. Warburg, O., F. Wind, and E. Negelein, "The Metabolism of Tumors in the Body." *J Gen Physiol*, 1927. 8(6): p. 519.

36. Katz, D.L. and R.S.C. Friedman, *Nutrition in clinical practice: a comprehensive, evidence-based manual for the practitioner.* 2nd ed. Philadelphia: Lippincott Williams & Wilkins, 2008.

37. Gardner, A., et al., "Randomized comparison of cooked and noncooked diets in patients undergoing remission induction therapy for acute myeloid leukemia." *J Clin Oncol,* 2008. 26(35).

38. van Tiel, F., et al., "Normal hospital and low-bacterial diet in patients with cytopenia after intensive chemotherapy for hematological malignancy: a study of safety." *Ann Oncol,* 2007. 18(6): p. 1080.

39. Pentecost, J.D. and J. Danilson, *The words and works of Jesus Christ: a study of the life of Christ.* Grand Rapids, Mich.: Zondervan Pub. House, 1981.

40. Ferguson, S.B., *The Christian life: a doctrinal introduction.* London: Hodder and Stoughton, 1981.

41. Pink, A.W., *The attributes of God.* New ed. Grand Rapids, Mich.: Baker Books, 2006.

42. *Health Information Privacy.* U.S. Department of Health and Human Services,

http://www.hhs.gov/ocr/privacy/hipaa/understanding/consumers/inde x.html.

43. *The Dohnavur Fellowship.* India Gateway, http://www.indiagateway.net/dohnavurfellowship/about.html.

44. Elliot, E., *A chance to die: the life and legacy of Amy Carmichael.* Old Tappan, N.J.: F.H. Revell Co., 1987. p. 319.

45. Carmichael, A., *Though the mountains shake.* 2nd ed. New York,: Loizeaux Bros, 1946 p. 13.

46. Powlson, D. *Don't Waste Your Cancer - Expansion of John Piper's Essay,* http://www.desiringgod.org/resource-library/taste-see-articles/dont-waste-your-cancer.

47. Smith, C.W., *Commencement Address,* G.C.o.T.M.s. College, Editor. 2002: Santa Clarita, CA.

48. Bunyan, J. and L.E. Hazelbaker, *The pilgrim's progress in modern English.* North Brunswick, NJ: Bridge-Logos Publishers, 1998.

49. *Heidelberg Catechism.* Westminster Theological Seminary, http://www.wts.edu/resources/creeds/heidelberg.html.

50. Spurgeon, C., *Morning and Evening: King James Version / A Devotional Classic For Daily Encouragement.* Peabody, Mass: Hendrickson Pub, 2010.